Essays
on the State
Legislative
Process

Essays on the State Legislative Process

DONALD G. HERZBERG
Eagleton Institute of Politics,
Rutgers—The State University of New Jersey

JESS UNRUH
Assembly of the State of California

HOLT, RINEHART AND WINSTON, INC.

New York   Chicago   San Francisco   Atlanta
Dallas   Montreal   Toronto   London   Sydney

This volume of essays is dedicated
to the Eagleton Fellows—
those that have been and those yet to be

Preface

The Eagleton Institute of Politics has in recent years become particularly involved in the study and reform of state legislatures. This volume of essays is a direct result of that involvement.

In 1963, Jess Unruh, then Speaker of the Assembly of the State of California, who had made many successful campus appearances around the country, spent a number of days at the Eagleton Institute as its politician-in-residence. It quickly became apparent to him and to members of the institute faculty that they shared a common concern for the future of state government in general and state legislatures in particular. That concern became translated into action. Mr. Unruh joined the Eagleton faculty as a continuing, visiting professor. He worked directly with the co-author, Donald G. Herzberg, Director of the Eagleton Institute, in teaching the Eagleton Fellows involved in the special graduate program designed to train young people for non-civil service positions in government and politics. Under his guidance an increasing number of Eagleton students upon graduation have taken positions working for state legislatures.

In addition, Mr. Unruh has assumed the "deanship" of the Eagleton Seminars for young state legislators. This program, under a grant from the Carnegie Corporation, brings together carefully selected legislators from all fifty states to discuss common problems and seek guidance of senior legislators and others

concerned about state legislatures. Mr. Unruh has also partici-
pated in a number of Eagleton studies of certain state legislatures,
under direct contracts from these legislatures, designed to recommend changes in procedures and operations that will make them
a more vital, coordinate branch of state government.

The chapters in this volume have been developed from two
sources: first, from the speeches Mr. Unruh has delivered on state
legislatures and their problems; and second, from speeches and
articles Professor Herzberg has written on specific problems of
state legislatures. In several of the latter, Dr. Alan Chartock of
the Eagleton Institute has acted as coauthor. Mr. Unruh's
speeches show great insight into the specific nature of legislatures,
and they also reflect his own accomplishments in transforming
the California Assembly into a governmental body that acts
responsibly and responsively to meet the changing needs of the
state. In translating his speeches into essays, Professor Herzberg
has tried to retain the flavor of these accomplishments.

State governments *can* be reformed and state legislatures
can become responsive, democratic, progressive institutions.
These essays discuss problems, but they do not attempt to present
panaceas—rather, they pinpoint some of the more crucial areas
in need of reform.

The authors' emphasis is on California, primarily because
Mr. Unruh is so integrally involved in California political reform,
and secondly because California has made obvious strides toward
viable legislative reform. The authors do not intend to slight or
ignore any other state involved in reform; they merely are speaking of those areas where they have most expertise.

The approach of this volume is dictated by the combination
of the authors' political and academic background and experience. They have both been closely involved with the political
system, one as a participant, the other as a concerned observer.
Because of this association with the state legislative process they
feel they are in a position to speak of those problems and those
reforms that they believe will enable the state legislatures to do
the job demanded for the 1970s.

Chapter 4—An Attempt to Innovate: The California Federal Legislative Office—digresses from the usual pattern of the
essays. It describes in detail an innovation in state government
successfully implemented by California. It is included for its detail, originality, and subsequent success of the liaison approach
to state government.

In their work of developing these speeches and articles into essays the authors have been aided immeasurably by research assistants Lisa Fairman Heher and Jennefer Verdini. The authors are both deeply in their debt. Mrs. Heher began the task of organizing the speeches and casting them into essays, while Miss Verdini finished that task and also suggested the manner in which the essays should be organized. The authors are also indebted to Sally Runyon, a professional member of the staff of Eagleton's Legislative Center, who did much of the editing, and to Karen Osowski, who typed the manuscript.

D.G.H.
J.U.

New Brunswick, New Jersey
Sacramento, California
August 1970

Contents

PART ONE

The Challenge: Modernizing the State Governments

Today state legislatures are the "emerging nations" of American politics. For decades they have been ignored by the public and the press except on those occasions when their members did something particularly venal or stupid. At the same time they were disdained by all but a handful of political scientists as unworthy of study. Now, suddenly, attention is specifically being focused on state legislatures as it is being directed at state governments in general. It is no longer out of fashion to be a specialist in state government. There is general agreement among political observers that American state government is in crisis.

State governments now are overwhelmed by the demands put upon them by the needs of their citizens. The complexities of our society, the crises of our cities, and the rising costs of government have overtaxed the fiscal resources of the states while public requests for the state to spend more on education, to build more roads, to modernize institutional facilities, and to enlarge welfare programs have increased. Many observers predict that soon the states of the United States will become mere appendages to the federal government, or worse yet, ignored by a national government that deals directly with the urban areas of the nation, bypassing the states entirely.

State governments were not always so troubled. At one time it was not unusual for American government textbooks to describe the states as the laboratories of American democracy. States had been the testing ground for the programs that comprised much of the New Deal. Unemployment insurance, minimum wage provisions, and regulations of health and safety in mining and industry, for example, were all adaptations of state experiments. Since the New Deal legislation in 1933, however, there has been a steady, relentless erosion of state authority and a parallel decline in state responsibility. The states in general have not demonstrated that they can do the job, and consequently public confidence in them has been severely shaken.

Part One elaborates on the kinds of problems confronting state legislatures and offers an alternative to the pessimistic diagnosis of many political analysts that the states are dead. We *know* that the future for state government is uncertain and that the road back to state responsibility will not be an easy one. However, we do not believe the task impossible. Just as whole nations have been modernized, so too state legislatures can be modernized to meet the challenges of a highly advanced industrial society.

CHAPTER ONE

State Legislatures at the Crossroads

The challenge to the American states to play both their constitutional and humane role in the federal system is immediately upon them. Because of pressing social and political problems, states are likely to be participating in vast new programs and greatly enlarged old ones. This participation will become quite complicated if and when federal tax money is rebated to the states. How the states deal with these federal monies, given with fewer federal strings attached, will determine the fate of state government for the next decades. If they prove to be unimaginative and inflexible, then state governments may end up as mere appendixes of our governmental system. If, on the other hand, state governments act imaginatively, and prove to be responsible as well as responsive to the needs of their citizens, then Americans will be able to witness a golden age of federalism. Furthermore, Americans will have proven that a complex and diverse society with a larger population dispersed over a wide geographic area can be governed successfully.

Source: This essay is taken from *Our State Legislatures: They Are at a Crossroads,* a "Grass Roots Guide" written by Donald G. Herzberg and Alan S. Chartock. The guide was published in 1969 by the Center for Information on America, Washington, Connecticut, and is used by permission.

At the heart of the issue—whether state government will respond responsively or not—are fifty state legislatures and the thousands of legislators. Of the three branches of state government, state legislatures are the least known and least understood. Yet, it is a fact that state legislatures play an essential part in regulating the lives of the citizens of the state and in determining what kind of a life they shall lead.

Knowledge of the way in which state legislatures in the United States are organized and perform is essential to anyone believing in democracy. With the expanding role of state government, the legislature will have more and more responsibilities. As of now, most state legislatures have not developed the resources necessary for designing, implementing, and overseeing the operation of state programs. Programs of tax sharing or "block-grants" to the states from the national government may soon be a reality. One popular concept of representative government is that the state legislators should *re-present* the views of their constituents. Constituents, it is thought, should make known their wishes to their legislators who in turn should turn them into public policy. According to this theory, if a constituent is not satisfied with the performance of his elected representatives, he should vote against them; if he is satisfied, he should support them at the polls.

As we know, this theory often breaks down. For example, political scientists tell us that on many occasions, the way in which the individual votes is affected by variables such as the political affiliation of the voter's parents rather than by the performance of his representatives on particular issues such as health or tax policy. We know, furthermore, that many individuals consider politics a dirty game, corrupt, and incomprehensible. Yet, these same individuals often do not believe that there is anything they can do about improving what they consider a discouraging situation and resign themselves to a political system that they feel is inadequate. Thus, we know that many Americans' interest in politics often stops at the voting booth if indeed it gets that far. Many of the very groups that need to be heard by lawmakers have completely lost faith in the legislative process. They believe that the system is so irresponsible that it cannot possibly be utilized to achieve social and political change. The result is often frustration, which leads in turn to other ways of attaining desired changes.

In an age where "ombudsmen" and "increased communication" are fast becoming everyday words, it seems incredible that our legislatures have not opened every available avenue to solicit the ideas of minority groups. In part this is the fault of legislatures that operate in closed and executive sessions. It has been demonstrated in states such as Wisconsin that legislatures can meet in open session, with the press present, and still conduct their business with a high level of effectiveness.

Lack of participation by many citizens and organizations makes it comparatively easy for organized interest groups to make their mark on the legislative process. Time and again it has been demonstrated that a few knowledgeable individuals have the capacity to successfully undertake a particular campaign in the state legislature for the enactment of a legislative proposal. Conversely, the vast majority of persons who sit on their hands for one reason or another are deprived of a say in making state policy. Legislators are not always informed on both sides of an issue. If there is no evident opposition to a particular bill, it becomes much easier for the bill's proponents to see it through the legislature. In this way, many inferior bills have been successfully negotiated through the legislative process.

The lack of human communication is never more evident than in the problem of scarce citizen participation in the legislative process. Partly because of this lack of interest and partly because of a tendency of some of those in power to prefer limited political participation, the state legislature has failed to equip itself to handle the complex problems of American life. Solutions to the problems of the cities, education, health, sanitation, housing, agriculture, and prisons are often outside the competency and ability of the legislature.

THE LEGISLATIVE TASKS

The legislature has several tasks. These are the *initiation* of new legislation, the legislature's *oversight* of the bureaucracy, and the *servicing of constituent governmental problems*. In recent years, the legislature typically has not initiated major legislation. Because of the complexity of modern government, the task of designing new programs has fallen in large part to the bureaucracy; it is developed within the executive branch, which has the manpower and expertise to design the complicated new programs. The legislature only sees the new program after the bureaucracy and key persons in the governor's office have devoted large amounts of time to the issue.

The problem here is that the legislator is then put into a position of saying *yes* or *no* to a program, or of modifying it. Seldom is he thinking out creative new alternatives to those solutions proposed by the government agencies. If a new health, education, or welfare program is designed by government agencies, there is very little that the legislator can do but to modify, reject, or accept that program. In order to create new programs the legislature would have to employ experts in each of the different substantive fields, such as education, health, and welfare.

Certain legislatures, such as the United States Congress and the California Assembly, have developed specialized staffs, and these bodies have themselves been responsible for initiating major new governmental programs. Of course, it is not impossible for the legislature to initiate legislation. An interested individual or interest group often comes to strategic legislators with a bill or a series of bills for introduction. If the legislator believes the ideas have merit, he may direct his staff or the legislative reference service in his legislature to embody the idea into bill form. Nevertheless, the legislature does not initiate most major legislation.

THE LEGISLATOR AND THE BUREAUCRACY

While the legislature has declined in potency, state executive agencies have been increasingly instrumental in the process of policy making in the states. In this regard, the management bureaucracies have taken over functions that were traditionally discharged by the governor and the legislature. In fact, bills that affect state executive agencies by giving or taking away responsibilities are often drafted by the very same agencies that the legislation affects. Furthermore, agency administrators are considered to be most expert in different policy areas and are given great respect for that reason.

What all this means is that the bureaucracy often becomes the major decisional force in state policy making. Persons wishing to influence public policy often go directly to the bureaucracy, rather than the legislature. The governor in many states, principally through his budgetary apparatus, has developed machinery that he can at least keep up through the bureaucracy. The legislature, however, has failed to provide itself with the appropriate machinery that can, at least, enable it to oversee the policy-making process.

The legislature has to provide itself with the resources necessary to do its job. Experts agree that these resources include increased information staff, physical facilities, and increased use of the legislative committees.

LEGISLATIVE OVERSIGHT

Although legislatures have de-emphasized their initiatory function, their function of oversight of the bureaucracy has continued. Oversight encompasses those activities undertaken by the legislature to ensure that the state government is running properly and complying with requirements of legislative programs. With the growth of state bureaucracies, legislatures are handicapped in providing oversight of the entire bureaucratic apparatus. The increased technical and detailed aspects of today's programs also make oversight functions difficult. These problems of oversight are made even more complex by federal program requirements and problems of implementation at the state level, by metropolitan and local programs, and by interestate and regional compacts and agreements. Without sophisticated staff and well-organized functional committees, the outlook for legislative oversight is bleak indeed.

THE COMMITTEE SYSTEM

The committee system is a device for enabling legislators to study and review the content of legislative proposals. Committees are also used for oversight, for fact finding, and for appraisal of program implementation by the state bureaucracy. Committees may be set up within a legislature to operate only during the legislative sessions or when not in session or during the members' entire term of office. The fact that many committees of the legislature overlap considerably makes for confusion in the legislative process. Because the jurisdictional responsibility of different committees is diffuse, research and oversight is similarly chaotic. For this reason, the committee system, in many state legislatures, is ineffective. Because of a proliferation of committees, major responsibility is often placed in a single committee, while others fall into a state of decay. This means that only a few legislators will have major responsibilities.

Often, the legislature's finance committees are the focal points of the committee systems in state legislatures. The leadership of the important finance committee may be chosen on the basis of past performance or as a result of an election for speaker or majority leader. They may receive a higher salary than the rank-and-file legislators and are included in the legislative leadership. In comparison to other standing committees, the staffing of the finance committee also reflects the powerful position of this committee in the legislature. Although few, if any, standing committees of most legislatures are staffed on a year-round basis, the finance committees enjoy this kind of year-round resource, often making them crucial decision makers within the legislative process. Frequently legislative finance committees are staffed with competent personnel on the same basis as the governor's office, for the purpose of overseeing and evaluating the expenditures of state funds.[1]

Of the fifty legislatures within the United States, only a few have anything approaching an effective legislative committee. According to Belle Zeller:

> It is generally recognized that the existing committee system of most state legislatures is poorly constituted to handle the large volume of important legislation. In practically all states, there are too many standing committees in each house, resulting in some cases, in needless duplication, confusion, waste of legislative talents, and the absence of each committee for legislation in its own field.[2]

If the committee system in the legislature is to function effectively, there must be a limited number of committees that can be staffed, manned, and funded with the resources available to each legislature. According to an American Assembly report, "State legislatures should not permit the unhealthy proliferation

---

[1] See Alan Chartock, "Mental Health Policy-Making in Three American States: A Study in Political Behavior" (Ph.D. thesis, New York University, 1968), pp. 73–78.

[2] Belle Zeller, *American State Legislatures* (New York: Thomas Y. Crowell, 1954), p. 95.

of standing committees." [3] The report states that the optimum number of committees is somewhere between ten and fifteen and that serious efforts should be exerted to keep down the number of committee assignments each legislator is asked to shoulder.[4]

Since informational resources and expert sources of advice are concentrated in the management agencies, legislative committees tend to rely on the resources of the bureaucracies for oversight (that is, they tend to believe what the bureaucracies tell them), for policy initiation, and for political favors. As a result, conflicts may emerge. Lines of executive authority may be blurred and confused, and a committee chairman may go as far as to extend his role to give direction to departmental policy. This may damage the relationships of the governor with the agencies, the governor's relationships with the legislature, and the agency's own standing in relation to the legislature.

Advocates of legislative reform have suggested that the legislature require mechanisms for developing alternative policies to those of the operating departments. They argue that the legislature must equip itself with the resources necessary to do this work. However, counterarguments criticizing this ambitious approach as "too expensive" are voiced by opponents of reform. Nevertheless, advocates of reform argue that corrective measures must be taken. One proposal for achieving this result is through strengthening the staff work of standing committees.[5] According to William Keefe and Morris Ogul, "The hard facts concerning employment of professional committee staffs by state legislatures suggest that the matter is regarded as one of low urgency." [6] Ap-

[3] American Assembly, "Our State Legislature: Prospects and Problems" (Conference held at Tulane University, Baton Rouge, La., on January 26–29, 1967), p. 12.
[4] American Assembly, "Our State Legislature," p. 12.
[5] For discussions of increased committee responsibilities see the following series of books published by Rutgers University Press, New Brunswick, N.J.: Alan Rosenthal, *Strengthening the Maryland Legislature* (1968); David Ogle, *Strengthening the Connecticut Legislature* (1970); Charles Tantillo, *Strengthening the Rhode Island Legislature* (1968); and Alan Chartock and Max Berking, *Strengthening the Wisconsin Legislature* (forthcoming).
[6] William J. Keefe and Morris S. Ogul, *The American Legislative Process: Congress and the States* (Englewood Cliffs, N.J.: Prentice-Hall, Inc., 1963), p. 203.

parently, this is a moot issue, and some of the staff resources available to legislators are worthy of discussion.

THE LEGISLATIVE COUNCIL

Closely aligned with the committee system in many states is the legislative council. Legislative councils often exist as a result of the fact that legislatures in some states meet only a few months every other year. Experts proposing reform for different legislatures have suggested that legislatures meeting infrequently should meet more often in order to consider pressing problems more closely. Consequently, increasing numbers of states are moving toward annual legislative sessions.

For this reason, the legislative council "idea" of a group of legislators charged with overseeing and researching important governmental problems during the interim between legislative sessions is in increasing disfavor. Nevertheless, in states where legislative councils do exist, citizens concerned with change in law should acquaint themselves with the operations of these important bodies. Committees established by legislative councils are often charged with major policy formulation roles. The products of these groups are then submitted to the full legislature for passage. It is noteworthy that many of the important decisions in the legislature are made by members of the legislative councils.

LEGISLATIVE REFERENCE BUREAU

Many people are unaware that one need not be a lawyer to participate in the legislative process. However, it is true that many state legislatures have a preponderance of lawyers. In numerous ways this is unfortunate, since the other professions are not represented in the same manner. For instance, having educators, physicians, journalists, and businessmen serve in the legislature would help supply useful information and expertise. The actual technical bill drafting that is done in the legislature is seldom performed by legislators themselves. Rather, it is the job of a specialized agency, often known as the legislative reference bureau. A member need only bring an idea or concept to the bill drafting service, and within the framework of their expertise, the bill drafters will frame proposed legislation. In some states a citizens' group may request that the bill drafting service frame the legislation for them.

Thus, once a group gets an idea, they can either have it drafted into bill form, or they can request that a legislator do it for them. Since relatively few persons realize this, many groups fail to take advantage of this service. Of course, the service and its quality vary from state to state. In some states, where the legislature does not have adequate bill drafting services, steps should be taken to strengthen the legislature.

LOBBYISTS

Legislators often rely on lobbyists to place needed ideas and information at the disposal of the legislature. Many legislators actively solicit ideas for new legislation from individual constituents with very little return. For example, one New York State legislator requested that groups concerned with mental health legislation send him ideas to be processed through the mental health committee of which he was chairman. The response was nominal. For this reason, those groups who do choose to make themselves heard on a particular issue often assume disproportionate influence. Again, the need for professional staffs in different fields of expertise is made clear. Staffs can ferret out information other than that supplied by the lobbyists and interest group personnel. Several states have "conflict of interest" and "ethics" legislation designed to help control excessive influence of the interest groups on the legislature. Unfortunately, such legislation sometimes has the effect of driving "conflict of interest" situations underground.

COMPENSATION

Closely connected with the influence of lobbyists on the legislature is the question of legislative compensation. Most state legislators are underpaid. Many states, compensating their legislators at a rate just slightly above the national average of $4375,[7] maintain that they are "better than other states" and should not

[7] Research and Policy Committee, *Modernizing State Government* (New York: Committee for Economic Development, July 1967), p. 81.

raise salaries. This is a spurious argument. In the opinion of Larry Margolis, Executive Director of the Citizens Conference on State Legislatures, there is no legislature in the United States that pays its legislators adequately.

Legislators deserve an executive salary since they are elected by the people of the state to make the most important decisions relating to the state. The job of the legislator is an extremely high-risk activity in that he may be removed from office at any time.

The Committee for Economic Development has stated that legislators should be paid at the rate of $25,000 per year in larger states, and at least $15,000 in other states.[8] A number of writers are disposing of the argument that legislators are part-time and should be paid as such. Responsibilities outside the capitol relating to constituents and preparation for the legislative session make the job of the legislator extremely demanding.

Even if legislators were to say that they spend 70 percent of their time on their legislative work, there is no guarantee that they would have enough energy or opportunity to find employment for the remaining 30 percent of their time. Legislators must be allowed a decent standard of living, rather than having to face continually the dilemma of deciding whether particular "outside" work constitutes a "conflict of interest."

Another argument advanced against increased legislative compensation is that legislators should not serve because of monetary reward, but because of a desire for serving the public and the government. However, according to a study published by the Citizens Conference on State Legislatures and the study of the Wisconsin Committee on Improved Expenditure Management, legislative pay compares unfavorably with the pay of other public officials, taking into consideration the time spent on the job. These studies demonstrated that the median annual salary of state legislators was well below that of congressmen, city aldermen, and other state government officials. Governors make $25,000; lieutenant governors, $9750; attorneys general, $19,500; secretaries of state, $16,000; executive secretaries to governors, $16,000; finance or administrative secretaries, $20,000; revenue or taxation secretaries, $17,500 and health department heads, $23,000.[9]

[8] Research and Policy Committee, *Modernizing State Government*, p. 39.
[9] *The Milwaukee Journal*, May 12, 1968.

If we are to expect legislators to react to the needs of their constituents, we must make increased resources available to them. The latter include resources that any business would consider essential. These are:

1.   Use of computers and improved research
2.   A private office for legislators where the constituent may speak freely and uninhibitedly to his legislator
3.   A telephone for each legislator with sufficient long distance allowances to keep in touch with his constituents
4.   A secretary to assist him in communicating with his constituents
5.   A research or administrative assistant to help develop a legislative program
6.   A car or mileage allowance which will allow the legislator to travel to meetings and to meet with constituents

FACING THE PROBLEM

The depressing condition of American state legislators has not gone unnoticed. Help properly has been assigned to the strengthening of state legislatures by concerned organizations such as the Carnegie Corporation, the Ford Foundation, the Eagleton Institute of Politics, the National Conference of State Legislative Leaders, the League of Women Voters, the Council of State Governments, and the American Assembly. Several state legislatures have been intensely examined by Citizens Commissions and professional consultants. The needs of each of these have been detailed and recommendations made. Many of these recommendations center around the problems already outlined in this chapter. They include better committees, more staffing, more office space, better pay, more modern machinery, better legislative services, and the recruitment of well-equipped candidates from all phases of political and social life.

Most of all, improved legislatures are dependent on an aroused citizenry. Time and again, a handful of individuals armed with positive suggestions for improvement have succeeded in upgrading and modernizing state legislatures. This is the area where many of the nation's most pressing social problems must be met. To continue to disregard the legislatures is political suicide.

CHAPTER TWO

Legislative Innovation and Resistance to Change

The people who lived in the Middle Ages probably thought they were modern. Disturbingly enough, Americans too think they are modern even in the face of occasional empirical evidence to the contrary. It would be well for us to remember the sage observation of the eighteenth-century physicist and philosopher Georg Christoph Lichtenberg: "Perhaps in time the so-called Dark Ages will be thought of as including our own."

A case might be made for characterizing the period of the last two generations as the Dark Ages of state legislatures, but hopefully this will be so temporary that posterity will consider this threat to the American system of constitutional federalism too inconsequential to record as history. This same period has demonstrated modern man's capacity to find imaginative solutions to previously unimagined problems, and the disease of legislative deterioration is not yet so far advanced that a cure is unthinkable. Indeed, in recent years many "doctors" have interested themselves in this "patient." State legislators are only now becoming accustomed to the probing and sympathy of political scientists and nonprofit foundations.

Source: Adapted from an address delivered by Jess Unruh at the Eagleton Seminar for Young State Legislators, Miami, Florida, August 7, 1966.

The desirable forms of legislative change have been discussed elsewhere. This chapter does not project into the future, but rather describes the unpleasant present—the forces of resistance to the legislative innovation that Americans endorse. Legislative change is opposed in this effort by the other branches of government, particularly the executive branch, as well as by the third house (lobbyists) and the special interests its members represent, and by the press. The most disturbing force in opposition to change, however, is that from within the legislature itself —the lack of vision among legislators that can frustrate change before it begins.

A brief allusion to the history of legislative inadequacy may serve as a spur to change. We are in difficult straits as a result of the moral indignation of another era. In the words of Finley Peter Dunne's famous characters:

"I don't like a rayformer," said Mr. Hennessey.
"Or anny other raypublican," said Mr. Dooley.[1]

Whether or not one agrees with Mr. Dooley's partisan contempt for the movement, it is clear that the reformers of his time effectively "threw the rascals out" of many governmental institutions including state legislatures. Unfortunately, they also created mechanisms and cultivated popular attitudes that tended to make legislative service difficult for "rascals"—or for anyone else, for that matter. This may account for Roscoe Conkling's epigram to the effect that "when Dr. Johnson defined patriotism as the last refuge of a scoundrel, he was unconscious of the undeveloped capabilities of the word 'reform.' " [2]

There is an old and respected basis for the theory that government is improved by weakening the legislative branch. James

---

[1] Finley Peter Dunne, "Reform Administration," *Observations by Mr. Dooley* (New York: R. H. Russell, 1902). The essay from which this quotation was taken appears in a collection of Dunne's essays entitled *Mr. Dooley on Ivrything and Ivrybody,* Robert Hutchinson, ed. (New York: Dover Publications, 1963). Finley Peter Dunne was a political satirist of the late nineteenth and early twentieth centuries, and Mr. Dooley, an Irish-American street-corner philosopher, was the character used most often to express Dunne's views on the Spanish-American War, Teddy Roosevelt, city government, women's rights, and other issues of his time. Mr. Dooley and his friend, Mr. Hennessey, were enormous popular favorites.
[2] Roscoe Conkling (1829–1888) was a long-time political leader and United States Senator and Representative from New York.

Madison, writing at the dawn of American federalism, speculated in *Federalist Paper* No. 51 about the effectiveness of our system of checks and balances and reflected this fear of a strong legislative branch:

> In Republican government, the legislative authority necessarily predominates. The remedy for this inconveniency is to divide the legislature into different branches; and to render them, by different modes of election and different principles of action, as little connected with each other as the nature of their common functions and their common dependence on the society will admit.

Madison goes on to say that the executive authority may require fortification at the expense of the legislative branch. He speaks of the veto power as a "natural defense," but suggests that it may not be enough. He also makes it clear that he is speaking both of state and federal governments.

Granting Madison's contention that state constitutions do not provide for the perfect separation of equal and distinct powers, it is clear that his fears for the executive branch of government are irrelevant for our time. The seeds of legislative weakness were indeed sown in those early state constitutions upon which Madison based his judgment. His inability to recognize them was a failing he shared with the other Founding Fathers. No one of that era could be expected to anticipate state governments of the magnitudes that exist today. But because these great men held the view that the executive branch must be fortified at the expense of the legislative, the opinion has become a tragically unexamined principle. As a result, the thirty-seven subsequent state constitutions of the American nation contain, to some degree, arbitrary restrictions on the legislative branch.

The fantastic growth of government has enhanced the power of the executive branch. The governor, because he is relatively free of procedural restraints, can adapt readily to new and expanding responsibilities. This necessity to accept new responsibility can blind the executives to the legislature's duty to study and refine the programs submitted to it, and its justifiable inclination to originate its own programs. Almost all of the practices that restrict the legislature work to the advantage of the governor.

The accretion of power in the administration is largely the result of its businesslike appearance. Power flows toward efficiency. People want the power they delegate to be used efficiently, and the efficiency of the legislative process is far from obvious. The legislature seems to exhaust its power in internal dissension, and the unsophisticated regard this as a waste. The ability to tolerate ambiguity is one of the indications of maturity, and American society has not reached a level of maturity that permits tolerance of the ambiguities in legislative decision making.

Legislative reform will not change the nature of executive operations nor diminish the inherent advantages of the office of governor. Legislative strengthening will not be accomplished at the expense of executive power, but it is extremely difficult to convince most governors of this. It is even more difficult to convince state executives of the advantages of legislative competition. The governor thinks of state agencies and departments as his, and while this attitude is probably good, it has implications that go beyond its usefulness in the executive branch.

Reasonably enough, administration agencies feel threatened by expertise that exists outside of the bureaucracy. The kind of expert staff that is essential to a modern, competitive legislature is just such a threat. Expert would be pitted against expert, and the probing policy questions would be asked, Is the department using the best possible methods? Is its budget too high? Is there any need for this department at all?

Finally, governors have something to gain in a short-run political sense from an outmoded, inadequate legislature. Talent that could provide political competition for the governor is not likely to be developed in an uninformed and dependent legislature.

The Jacksonian era, which brought the term "spoils system" into the American political lexicon, also coined the word "lobbyist." A few years later, Senator Thomas Hart Benton told a lobbyist that he would help him get a ship subsidy on the condition that "when the vessels are finished they will be used to take all such damn rascals as you, sir, out of the country." These opinions of the third house are still current. Only a few professions have persisted longer with such a poor public image, and politics rates at least a second place.

The special interest that lobbyists represent are acclimated to legislative weakness. They have influence in inverse ratio to legislative competence. It is common for a special interest to be the only source of legislative information about itself. The information that a lobbyist presents may or may not be prejudiced in favor of his client, but if it is the only information the legislature has, no one can really be sure. A special interest monopoly of information seems much more sinister than the outright buying of votes that has been excessively imputed to lobbyists.

As legislatures improve, the third house tends to improve too. The lobbyists, whose principal qualities have been talents for telling dirty stories and holding their liquor, are being replaced by articulate experts. But the change is taking place slowly; it lags far behind legislative innovation, which is itself quite laggardly.

Chambers of commerce and similarly oriented groups frequently pass resolutions urging citizens to actively work to improve government. The members of these groups could do much to accomplish this goal by improving the quality of their representation in state capitols. No one denies the third house its proper role, but unless its quality improves, it will be and should be ignored by a strong, independent legislature. An improved legislature will have no use for the old style lobbyist.

Although we think of them as dealing primarily with legislatures, lobbyists also influence the executive branch of government, and often this is a most expeditious course for them to follow. Many businesses are parties to "sweetheart" contracts with the executive branch in an unseemly arrangement for mutual exploitation. The mass membership groups, like labor unions, senior citizens, government employees, and even college professors, are willing to settle for increases in the size of their government checks rather than hard, substantive improvements.

The simplest, quickest, and easiest route to success for groups so motivated is through the governor's office. It is to their advantage if he alone has the staff and facilities to provide leadership. Unchallenged by the other branches, the executive need do little more than satisfy the common desires of enough people to get reelected. Without commenting on the quality of leadership that this situation can produce, it should be clear that lobbyists have a stake in reinforcing the governor's resistance to legislative change.

If it is difficult to impress the governor with the advantages of legislative competition, it is all but impossible to convince the press of those advantages. Generally, coverage of state legislatures is extremely superficial even if all-inclusive. So-called in-depth reporting is celebrity oriented and, therefore, often unproductive. It is as if no policy issues existed in the policy-making branch of government. A press that only deplores the sad condition of the legislature without reporting why the condition exists can hardly be expected to support improvements or even recognize what changes are needed other than "better legislators."

An uncooperative press is only one of the barriers to developing popular support for legislative innovation. The people themselves have a natural resistance to change in their governmental institutions, particularly when those changes involve strengthening government. A passionate defense of the principles of the Founding Fathers informs the arguments of liberals and conservatives alike. This is a nation of traditionalists when it comes to government, and even *proposals* for change are enough cause of suspicion.

The concept of government as a continually evolving entity is bewildering to the public. Organizational questions are never resolved with any finality, and this makes people confused and angry. One need only cite the current, often acrimonious debate over the proper role of the courts to illustrate this point. The advocate of legislative reform must recognize that, as far as the public is concerned, he is just another incomprehensible specialist tampering with government, and probably not to be trusted. Under the present circumstances, we cannot expect intense public concern about the status of legislatures.

In his book *The Phantom Republic*, Walter Lippmann offers the following appraisal of the role of public opinion in government:

> The work of the world goes on continually without conscious direction from public opinion. At certain junctures problems arise. It is only with the crises of some of these problems that public opinion is concerned. And its object in dealing with a crisis is to help allay that crisis.
>
> I think this conclusion is inescapable. For though we may prefer to believe that the aim of popular action should be to do justice or promote the true, the beautiful, and the good, the belief will not maintain itself in the face of plain experience. The public does not know in most crises what specifically is the truth or the justice of the case, and men are not agreed on what is beautiful and good. Nor does the public rouse itself normally at the existence of evil. It is aroused at evil made manifest by the interruption of a habitual process of life. And finally, a problem ceases to occupy attention not when justice, as we happen to define it, has been done but when a workable adjustment that overcomes the crisis has been made.[1]

[1] Walter Lippmann, *The Phantom Republic* (New York: Harcourt, 1925), pp. 66–67.

State legislative ineffectiveness is the habitual pattern of life at present. If the problem of legislative inadequacy ever reached a point of crisis of sufficient magnitude to arouse public opinion, it would be too late to salvage the legislature as a working branch of state government. Short of total inaction—the refusal even to give the governor laws he could veto—what could the legislature do to produce a massive popular response favorable to the cause of reform? In this case, the remedy is definitely worse than the disease.

Although it is difficult to mobilize public opinion on behalf of legislative reform, the people's interest in the process cannot be ignored. Legislative changes must be accomplished publicly and candidly. At any stage of development, the public must be able to inform itself of legislative actions and goals. This is essential to the achievement of public confidence in whatever changes are made.

Legislators should admit to a tendency toward secretiveness in dealing with their own condition. Outside of the statutory context, this attitude is justifiable. The legislature is the embattled branch, and a defensive response is natural. But if we argue that legislative reform is in the public interest, then we cannot afford to be cryptic in accomplishing it. Legislators may have to endure uninformed criticism, they must not justify it by their actions.

As we stated before, the most formidable obstacle to legislative innovation is found within the legislature itself. Many legislators have come to regard their lack of professionalism as a positive virtue. The concept of the part-time citizen-legislator is attractive to some practitioners of the art. It implies both an identification with the people and a selfless dedication to good government. But we ought to have the humility to see that this idea is also tinged with aristocratic arrogance. The machinery of modern government is too intricate to be run by dilettantes.

During debate in the California Legislature on revising the legislative article of the state constitution, an argument was advanced that a full-time, full-salaried legislature would be nothing more than another governmental bureaucracy. To be sure, this can happen partially, but only if Americans let it. Bureaucracy is the governor's "albatross," and perhaps that is unavoidable. However, it can be avoided in the legislative branch. A higher degree of professionalism need not make Americans less responsive to their constituents. Legislators will be regarded as bureaucrats only when they think of themselves as bureaucrats, just as now they are considered incompetent and inconsequential largely because that is basically how they consider themselves.

There is another reason for legislator resistance to reform that is far less logical. Unlike the other branches of government, the legislature has a definite social atmosphere. Mutual respect and the sense of common purpose are the very substance of legislative activity. It is natural, then, that Americans begin to regard the legislature as a kind of exclusive club with unwritten rules and customs which all members respect; this can be a productive atmosphere in which to work.

The problem arises when this fraternal attitude becomes all-pervasive, and membership in the club becomes more important than membership in the legislature. Most Americans have encountered legislators of several years experience who are antipathetic to legislative innovation because of a vague feeling that the "new boys" should have to undergo the same hardships as the older members of the club. This is similar to saying that before a person can drive a car he must first drive a horse and buggy for a few years. The mere realization that this unreasonable attitude exists should mitigate its influence.

If experience sometimes creates resistance to legislative innovation, it can also improve the quality of legislators. The problem is that legislative experience on the state level is very expensive both in terms of money and political ambition. If the office of state legislator were more prominent, and the salary made commensurate, it would unquestionably retain more members. Americans would be buying time, which would improve legislative quality, although it would not *necessarily* do so. In the legislative branch more than any other, the precious resource of time can be wasted on useless partisan exercise. The famous former Speaker of the House Thomas Brackett Reed was once asked by a frustrated and indignant Democrat what he thought the rights of the minority party were. His answer was a trenchant summary of his own view of legislative leadership: "The right of the minority is to draw its salaries, and its function is to make a quorum." In those days of powerful Speakers, it was not only possible, but realistic for Reed to make a comment like that and to add the somewhat more philosophical observation, "The best system is to have one party govern and the other party watch."

Today Speaker Reed's kind of frank partisanship, whether we like it or not, is out of fashion. Indeed, it can be disastrous for the effort to upgrade state legislatures. The success of any legislative modernization effort depends upon the groundwork that is laid. Anything that fragments and factionalizes is destructive. If, for example, the thrust for reform comes principally from one house, it is all but impossible to overcome the apathy or open hostility of the executive branch.

The bipartisan approach is even more necessary if there is the obstacle of constitutional revision to overcome. Too many people already regard the state legislature as a place for trivial controversy, to be suffered rather than encouraged. If legislators cannot present a united front in an appeal for public support for their own institution, then it would be much better to postpone or abandon a campaign for reform, or at least to adopt a piecemeal approach.

Furthermore, the appeal for financial support for such a campaign must be made to those interests closest to the legislature. Generally, these interests take an extremely narrow view of legislative reform. As does the governor, the third house tends to believe that an increase in legislative competence somehow diminishes its own effectiveness. The complete dedication of leaders of both parties in both houses is required to overcome these feelings. It can be fatal to permit outside forces to whipsaw a legislature internally while it is engaged in a campaign on its own behalf.

Still other sources of important support in the public appeal for legislative reform are the so-called good government groups such as the League of Women Voters, National Municipal League, and so on. Usually, these groups demand bipartisanship.

Having emphasized the need for bipartisanship, it now becomes necessary to say something about how to achieve it, which is not easy. In many states, the Thomas Brackett Reed approach to legislating is not an historical curiosity. There is often little more for the minority party to do than sit and watch the other party govern. The resulting sense of frustration is more likely to produce a desire for revenge than for reform. It is difficult to determine whether the arrogance with which majority party leadership handles the minority stems from shortsightedness or supreme overconfidence, but it is usually repaid in kind when the minority replaces the majority. A high degree of cooperation with the minority is not only far more productive but also much more comfortable for legislators of both parties.

The minority party in the legislature, with a governor of the majority party, is nearly useless if it is denied all the tools of quality decision making. Even if the governor is of the same political faith as the minority, the quality of the legislative product is immeasurably improved if the minority has independent staffing. It is an exaggeration to say that the gulf between the parties is not so great as the gulf between the executive branch and the legislative in every instance and on every issue; however, something similar is very nearly the case as a general rule. Except along broad philosophical or ideological lines, the interests of governors are rarely similar to those of members of their own party in the legislature.

Legislatures are already factional by design—so much so that they appear incompetent and uncertain at the best of times. When legislative leaders are constantly quarrelsome, it cannot help but add to this image of incompetence. Certainly, argumentation is unavoidable in the necessary confrontation of the issues, but it ought to be confined or closely related to the issues. Legislators should be aware of the risks involved in attacking another legislator on behalf of the governor. They must be certain of the accuracy of their statements and have a healthy skepticism of the motives of the governor. Many governors are more interested in seeing legislators fight than in the facts.

Once again, this situation can be ameliorated by adequate staffing. If legislators are not equipped with staff to scrutinize material provided by the executive, it is extremely unlikely that they can determine what is fact and what is fancy if the material involves anything but the simplest and most obvious kind of issue. This can be illustrated by a recent experience in the California Legislature. The governor accused a legislative leader of the opposite party of purposely stalling his economy program. The leader, who had an excellent staff, had a quick research job done, which revealed that only one of the governor's twenty-two cost-cutting proposals had been introduced in his house and that the rest were languishing in the other chamber. He dutifully (if somewhat gleefully) informed the press of the inanity of the governor's charge. The governor then prepared a countercharge and asked the leader of his own party in the same house to issue it. This leader refused on the grounds that his own independent staff research indicated that the governor was, indeed, wrong.

Had the legislative leader been incapable of doing the necessary research job and accepted the assertions of the governor, a member of his own party, he undoubtedly would have been trapped by the opposition party and a legislative wrangle would have ensued. In the short run, one legislator might have been exposed, but one must not discount the long-run damage this kind of uninformed dispute does to the legislature as a whole.

Clearly, the issues dialogue is immeasurably improved by minority party staffing. Useless partisan argument, etiher with the majority or the executive, or both, is lessened. With staff and facilities, the minority can move intelligently, dissect proposals of the majority, and offer constructive amendment rather than simple obstinate obstruction. It also has a continuing involvement in the legislative process because of its capacity to originate its own proposals. Independent staffing also has its effect upon minority-majority cooperation. When each party can participate jointly in the origination and development of a program and feel it has a stake in it, not only is the program's legislative road smoothed, but gubernatorial hostility is neutralized.

Understanding the necessity for a drastic departure in dealing with the problem of hard-core unemployment, the majority leadership in Califorinia undertook an extensive staff study recently. As this study was progressing, it was discovered that the minority staff was also concerned with this issue and had started some work of its own on the same problem. Quite naturally, the two staff projects merged and a fruitful liaison developed.

At this point, the leadership of both parties faced a necessity for choice. Each could go its separate way and develop its own program. The minority program would face the opposition of the majority, and the majority program would face the hostility of the governor. This, of course, is not all bad. Criticism and compromise could have improved whichever program survived, but in this conflict atmosphere, the odds were against any program surviving.

Instead, both staffs concentrated their efforts on producing one bipartisan package of legislation. As soon as these bills were introduced, they received the full support of the governor. So solid was the support for the program that it was able to survive the opposition of the U.S. Department of Labor. To be sure, neither party can now claim full credit for what will be an effective new employment program in California, but the sacrifice of a little glory and a few headlines is a small price to pay for forward-looking legislation.

If both majority and minority leaders recognize the primacy of their obligation to make the legislative process work, not only is it productive, but it is also simply a comfortable way to work. Legislative efficiency is never an important concern of the executive except, perhaps, for publicity purposes. In fact, legislative efficiency is more likely to be contrary to the governor's desires. No one else will be concerned with the legislative function if the leaders are not. Beyond a doubt, that function is enhanced by adequate facilities and staff. Generally, these resources will only be available in an atmosphere of mutual concern, cooperation, and respect between majority and minority leadership.

Insofar as the relationship between the leadership and other legislators is concerned, change must take place here also. Old systems of patronage and punishment to impose discipline are largely irrelevant. A new discipline based upon knowledge and competence can be anticipated. Equipped with facilities and staff, majority and minority leaders would be excellent sources of information for the members of their houses. They would be able to formulate policy intelligently and independently. The knowledge they command, and the capacity to act and react quickly and accurately, would be the tools with which the leadership would maintain this new legislative discipline.

Additionally, good staffing would free the leadership of concern with policy details and routine data analysis. The leaders would have more time to do the work of leadership—formulating broad policy, dealing directly with colleagues, and handling parliamentary procedure. This, after all, is what legislative leaders are elected to do. All of this, of course, assumes a context of continuing legislative improvement in all respects. There are a few things that leadership can evolve which add materially to the efficacy of the legislative performance.

First, there is the question of involvement of those individual members who, if not frustrated and driven out of the legislature by rigid and unconcerned leadership, can add materially to the process. Leadership should constantly be on the watch for the relatively few gifted people that the elective process supplies to the legislature and attempt to reward them even if their views vary considerably from those of the leaders. This will necessitate elimination or modification of the seniority system or tradition, but the rewards of having intelligent, concerned, and committed secondary leadership are great. Not the least of these is better treatment by the communications media and subsequent easing of the obstacles to legislative reform.

Second, there is a need for legislative leadership to adhere rigidly to the rules of the house, both written and understood. The temptation for the minority to deviate from those rules because they are generally formulated to fortify the majority can be lessened by consultation with minority leadership during the formative period. The penalty for not doing this can be session-long wrangling and subsequent harm to the legislative image. Conversely, if the minority leadership is given reasonable participation, one should expect them to resist the temptation to use those rules as an excuse for irresponsibility. The need for the majority leadership to avoid shortcuts and to subscribe rigidly to the rules as agreed to cannot be exaggerated. Variations, which are necessary once in a while, should only be resorted to after agreement with the minority leadership.

It goes almost without saying that leadership has the responsibility for seeing that the work flow is relatively constant and evenly divided, that the calendar is kept moving, and trivia on the floor kept to a minimum. Floor debate should be confined as much as possible to major substantive bills. Decorum on the floor will be encouraged if the time spent on minor matters is reduced to a minimum. A consent calendar to eliminate unnecessary motions on the floor has been helpful to some legislatures. Better attention to the details of smoothing out the floor operation will improve the overall impression that the legislature creates and will make major changes more acceptable.

Curiously, whether a legislator is more interested in representing his district, boosting his party, helping the "old folks," or advancing his own political fortune, he can do any and all of these things better if he has first "helped the legislature"—helped it to raise its decision-making ability, to scrutinize, to originate, to innovate, to ask the right questions, and to grope with more insight for better settlements.

State legislatures should be developed and recognized as a meeting place, as a place of negotiation, and as a place for developing understanding among the people. State legislatures, through their methods of operation and the manifestation of knowledgeable concern with modern problems, can do much to relieve the anxiety and sense of frustration experienced by more and more Americans. This was the intent of the framers of the American system of representative democracy. It is the American responsibility and opportunity today.

CHAPTER THREE

The State
of the Legislative Art

The legislative process has changed very little over the years. Modern techniques—all so prevalent in business and in the executive branch—have not been adopted by the state legislatures. There is a wealth of scientific, academic, and business talent in the United States, and the state legislatures are not availing themselves of these resources. Even in the instances in which business acumen, analytic competence, and technical talent are available to government, it is often abused or not used at all.

The political process of the legislative art needs buttressing in terms of ability to study and judge the enormous spending programs presented for consideration. The major ingredients of government improvement must come from more effective recruitment, organization, and utilization of scientific talents in the service of government decision making.

Government could profit greatly by emulating the "result" orientation of private enterprise. The "profits" to be derived from a greater concern for results would show on the state ledgers as improved service at lower cost per unit. With the tremendous increase in the American population and with the commitment

Source: Adapted from an address delivered by Jess Unruh at the Eagleton Seminar for Young State Legislators, Miami, Florida, August 19, 1967.

to a high level of governmental service, Americans are going to have to find some kind of breakthrough in governmental costs and procedures so that (apart from direct payments) the services that are provided to growing numbers of citizens can be provided at a lower unit cost. Unless Americans can come up with something comparable to the technological breakthroughs of the industrial revolution and translate them into a lower unit cost for any governmental services, we are not going to be able to provide all of the services that American society needs at a feasible price.

The use of science and management skills by government has been implemented more fully within the federal executive establishment than at any other level of government. The complexities of budgeting for weapons systems design and procurement, problems of the peacetime uses of the atom, and plans for effective federal support of health research, are typical of problems of governmental policy that demand both scientific fact and sophisticated analytic devices as elements of their statement, consideration, and solution.

Given the enormous scope of federal influence and the inextricable involvement of technical questions with policy formulation, it is not surprising that "big" government, "big" science, and "big" business have nurtured each other. Although many problems of state and local government have technical components analogous to problems at the federal level, there are few analogies at the state and local levels of government to the Advisory Committee to the Atomic Energy Commission or to the various formally established scientific panels within most of the senior echelons of federal executive departments.

Much of the fault and remedy for the misallocation and poor utilization of scientific and managerial resources appears to lie with local governmental bodies. There are often cases of smugness, anti-intellectual feeling, and narrow provincialism in county seats and state capitols. Beyond a few cases of active hostility to the more general use of science in government there lies a rather massive indifference to such use, grounded in ignorance of the use and results of technical advice.

The meager level of scientific participation in state government is unfortunate in *at least* the following four ways.

First, the lack of access to reliable technical opinion puts legislators, in particular, at a disadvantage in appraising the claims of special interest groups that can and do command expert advice. The problem of program appraisal by legislators is technically identical whether the program is a water development plan proposed by the governor or an amendment to the agriculture code proposed by a chemical manufacturers' association. In both cases, the only facts, measurements, and estimates of consequences available to the legislature are those presented by the proponent of a program.

In some cases, when competitive forces are at work, there *may* be available a set of facts in rebuttal. The decision on which case, if any, is technically sound is left to inexpert legislators reacting to normal and well-known lobby influences, Too often it is unaided by any independent capacity to identify relevant facts, to evaluate evidence, or to draw scientifically responsible and logically valid conclusions. This lack of access to independent advice puts local legislative bodies at an immediate political disadvantage in dealing with private interests and with certain types of executive proposals. Theoretical checks and balances, to be meaningful and productive, require that legislatures have a broader and more sophisticated capacity to acquire information and analyses in forms appropriate for use by legislators.

A second major constraint on the quality of state legislative performance, resulting from imperfect access to technical talent, involves the range of responses of which the legislature is capable. In normal practice, legislative committees can say *yes* by a do pass recommendation, *no* by killing an item in committee, or *maybe* by referral to interim study. The full legislative body has essentially the same set of options. On budget items the options are comparably narrow: *yes, no,* or *compromise* on a specific line item or specific program proposal.

With the exception of occasional uses of the tactic of bill amendment, legislatures are generally limited to these few, crude, all-or-none responses to questions formulated elsewhere in the structure of government. The capacity of legislatures to deal with alternatives, with gradations of support, or with problems of inter-program coordination, are limited by the form in which questions are put to legislative bodies. Even more crucially, they are restricted by limited independent capacity to design program alternatives and, generally, to take a creative role in the formulation of policy questions to be debated.

The major legislative function is the reconciliation of interests. (The legislature is more a catchpool of ideas than a wellspring.) If taken in a strict sense, it may leave too much to the haphazard processes that generate proposals and programs for legislative action and too little scope for the creative powers of synthesis that are often found among more able legislators. Substantially improved technical resources would give legislatures more effective means to evaluate, for example, the completeness of coverage of a governor's program, and, if need be, to design programs to fill in the gaps.

A third legislative limitation is due at least in part to inadequate professional support; this is the difficulty of dealing with governmental problems having long lead times and long time spans. Some of these difficulties stem from legislative turnover and the limited results from it; others stem from the reluctance of some legislators and of even more governors to "borrow trouble," that is, to talk about the effects of a proposed program in the years ahead when conceivably, somebody else, or the other party, may have to worry about tax increases which should be foreseen and prepared for at the start.

The few instances in which modern techniques of analysis have been applied to the elucidation of budgetary problems at the state level are impressive. If the will of the people is to be expressed through the votes of informed and judicious representatives, there will need to be a major increase in the contributions of specialists trained in the imaginative application of these impressive new analytic techniques.

There is no way to guarantee a high average level of individual competence among legislators, and it is far from obvious that the quality of government would necessarily improve by a massive improvement in the personal ability of all representatives. Perhaps a legislative body composed exclusively of highly talented, highly trained leaders might be less productive than legislatures with a more even distribution of talents.

In California some steps have been taken to improve the capabilities and effectiveness of legislators, but only as they arrive. The steps taken by the California Assembly include providing each assemblyman with an administrative assistant. These young people, often with graduate training in law, economics, political science, or journalism, take a major load of correspondence, fact finding, report drafting, and the like, from the assemblyman.

At the committee level, personnel of unusual abilities have been recruited to serve as staff members. During the sessions and during the interim periods, these consultants serve as executive officers to their chairmen in the management of committee business and concentrate their efforts in formal and informal research and fact finding. These staff positions are oriented to problem areas—public health, revenue and taxation, agriculture, and so on—rather than to the work of an individual legislator.

The California Assembly as a body has long been served by a large and well-staffed legal counsel office and by services from the Office of the Legislative Analyst, which acts as a legislative budget office.

Beyond these steps in staffing and in providing legal, bibliographic, and financial services, the California Legislature, following the example of business, is making increasing use of private consultants and research contractors. University faculties in particular have provided the legislature with some of their most distinguished advisers. So far, the principal use of leaders of the business community has been limited to boards and commissions designed to regulate their own spheres of activity. Occasionally, a blue-ribbon commission is created with a broad mandate to recommend new legislation in a troublesome field of general interest.

It is one thing to provide a legislature with expert staff and another for the legislators to take full advantage of experts and of the bodies of knowledge they represent. As one way of heightening the capabilities of legislators to use the contributions of scientists and scholars Jess Unruh initiated a series of two-day, live-in seminars for the members of assembly committees at the University of California at Berkeley. The university sent its best men in a given field (taxation in one case, urban problems in another) to give short summary papers in their fields and to participate in give-and-take discussions. The seminars were well attended and productive, both in the areas of heightened mutual respect and more discerning appreciation for the demands of political decision making and of the potential contributions of the academic disciplines to the improvement of these decisions.

In part, as a result of these "back to school" moves, many of the legislative committees have retained leading experts from the colleges and universities to advise them by preparing summaries of what might be called the "current state of the debate" on such complex questions as the regulation of utilities, or by briefing committee members in advance of hearings where complex technical testimony is to be presented. University faculties have provided the California Legislature with some of their most distinguished advisers—men like Professor Harold Somers, Chairman of the Economics Department at the University of California at Los Angeles, who assisted in the preparation of a major tax reform package designed to relieve the overburdened property owner.

The participation of faculty members as expert, neutral advisers in legislative deliberation is becoming more frequent.

This participation will undoubtedly produce both an atmosphere in which academic contributions are valued and sought and a heightened capability among legislators for using inputs of scientific fact and analysis as normal components of deliberations.

The academic world, however, represents only one category of expertise available to the legislature. Some of California's major business enterprises and some of its great labor organizations have done front-line work in long-range planning for economic development. There remains a need to fashion methods for the use of business and labor resources on public policy questions. This usage must be distinct from business and labor advocacy of particular programs in their immediate range of interests.

California has also instituted a plan to attempt to reduce the end of the session logjam of legislation and at the same time further improve the work of the interim committees. Under this plan the committees are asked to study and make recommendations on major issues and problems rather than simply evaluate bills and resolutions that were introduced during the previous session.

In improving the outputs from interim activities, the goal is not to spend less on interim activities but to produce more with the same input. Interim studies are viewed as devices for the following:

1. In-service training of new legislators
2. The design of increasingly comprehensive pieces of legislation
3. A method of carrying out a general function of legislative oversight into the workings of executive departments
4. An organized method for identifying gaps in the coverage, economy, and scope of governmental services

This focus on issues and problems, rather than on bills and resolutions, is the first step toward developing omnibus legislation. By encouraging committees to develop broad solutions to major problems and to draft committee legislation incorporating these solutions, it should be possible to reduce drastically the number of bills that need to be debated by the entire legislature. This reduction of the sheer number of items would, in turn, allow for much more thorough study of major bills by committees and for vastly expanded debate on the floor of the assembly.

One of the new lessons emerging from the effort to improve

legislative procedures relates to the unnatural fragmentation of subject matter. It is generally accepted that one of the toughest obstacles to social progress is the countless number of agencies that have been created over the years, each with its own territory to command and its own professional bias and rigidity. Legislative bodies have created complicated service systems that are often incapable of coping with the real world because their very design is at cross purposes with reality. To intensify this problem, the legislature in its "wisdom" has reflected *in its own structure* these identical and unrealistic separations. Thus we see social welfare, public health, budget, and tax committees each looking at the same issue (for example, medical care) from a different vantage point.

This structural weakness can be countered by more integrated research activities, not only through joint committee hearings on certain matters, but through an informal and effective technique of coordinated research on a staff level.

California's medical care program, for example, was formulated with extensive assistance from staffs of the Public Health, the Revenue and Taxation, Finance and Insurance, Ways and Means, and Social Welfare Committees. As this type of cooperation developed, the leadership learned the value of bringing together various skillful people with different professional backgrounds and no agency loyalties or dogmas to defend. These experiences paved the way for the creation of the Assembly Office of Research. This office was formed by converting and upgrading the old Legislative Reference Service and the Chief Consultant's Office into a single organization with a staff of professionals. It is possible to apply teams of experienced researchers to problems that cut across lines of committee responsibility or require more attention than the small committee staffs can give. Free of the day-to-day routine of committee work, these teams can devote as long and as intensive an effort as is required.

In addition to the development of this interdisciplinary style of work, it is necessary to develop more effective research within a political environment. It is not enough for legislative staff members to be technically competent, although this is an obvious prerequisite. The product is not a study report or publication in a prestigious professional journal. It is a law which must pass both houses and be signed by the governor. The legislative function demands the capacity to identify the most politically feasible alternative at any point in time.

For example, it might be logical and technically possible to study the economic and educational values of a single, state-operated school system for California as opposed to the value of maintaining hundreds of independent school districts. But even if such a study proved that a single state school system would be superior, the present political culture would make it impossible to pass the necessary legislation.

Just as it is a mistake to invest our limited time, energy, and money in projects that are clearly politically unrealistic, so it is also a mistake to be overly intimidated by what *appears to be* the political climate. Legislative studies themselves can have the effect of altering the way in which issues are perceived and can push past the boundaries of conventional wisdom. The proposal that may have been considered politically impossible prior to a research project may emerge as the only *politically* proper solution after a careful study has been made.

This apparent contradiction between the need to function within the boundaries of the politically possible and the need to push past those boundaries for imaginative solutions leads to a special style of legislative research. The research itself is used as a tool to test and to change the political climate. The legislative research project can have a unique capacity to alter the phenomenon being studied at the very moment that it is being studied.

Recently, the Assembly Transportation and Commerce Committee conducted a study of the smog problem in California that illustrates this point. The study included the following findings. Practically 90 percent of the problem in Los Angeles County and other major population centers comes from automobile exhaust; existing vehicle smog control measures are of limited value; if nothing new were done, the problem would become far worse within the next decade; smog is becoming a massive public health problem; the technology exists to reduce the problem significantly within a short time; and the primary obstacle to solving the problem is the powerful automobile industry.

This study, with the facts it uncovered, changed the very nature of the issue and the possibilities for legislative action. Just knowing the awful dimensions of the problem and knowing the available possible solutions allowed the consideration of legislation no one would have contemplated beforehand. Thus, this example shows how the legislative study can become a significant catalyst that may actually alter the political character of the problem by activating various conflicting vested interests and creating a more favorable climate for action.

Legislative studies differ from most academic research activities precisely because they are conducted by the legislature, a decision-making body. As a result, these studies have a vastly greater potential for immediately influencing action. Legislative studies are being conducted in public, and the various groups affected by the possible actions that a study may produce are generally concerned about the direction of the study even as it is being conducted. This concern allows the employment of valuable involvement and feedback techniques. Legislative studies of important issues can draw upon the information and viewpoints of all the vested interests in the community. It is possible for such a study to become a central forum for examining and debating a problem. The legislative study can be "where the action is" and, if properly conducted, can gather the most influential opinions and information from academic and other communities to produce a definitive analysis.

In some recent legislative studies in California, a deliberate attempt has been made to maximize this type of total public involvement through the use of the following techniques: asking various groups with conflicting views to provide information and testimony; asking interested organizations and industries to gather data for the study using questionnaires by legislative staff; distributing preliminary or tentative committee recommendations and structuring public hearings or mailing questionnaires to receive feedback and criticism; and even preparing rough drafts of actual legislation for submission to a cross section of the affected interests with the request that they criticize and draft alternative language.

When these techniques are used the legislature becomes less of an obstacle course for those interested in social change and more of a facilitating mechanism. It is possible to break through the barriers that separate the theorist from the decision makers. It can be demonstrated that a legislative body is capable of thinking as well as acting.

In ancient times and even in the early days of the United States, scholars and other men noted for great wisdom were frequently placed in legislative positions. In modern times the elected official is more often a person with whom the average citizen can identify and, in fact, there is a general suspicion of intellectualism. But Americans are learning the techniques of blending intellectual and pragmatic political functions in what may be an entirely new legislative style of work that holds great promise for the nation's legislatures.

PART TWO

The Significance:
A More Viable
Federal System

Our belief in the future of the states is not based on a blind, uncritical love of the past or a rigid status quo. The federal system of government devised by the Founding Fathers two hundred years ago is not necessarily perfect or perpetual. It is a system that is basically sound but which needs continual vigilance and overhaul. Our confidence in the future of the states is pragmatic. Our case is based on the proposition that it is exactly the complexity of twentieth-century life in the United States that makes state government uniquely qualified to solve the problems of its own citizens. In this day and age it is unrealistic to believe that broad solutions, no matter how broadly conceived in Washington, are necessarily the best solutions under the many circumstances that today prevail in states as far apart as Maine and Hawaii, and as different in character as Nevada and New York.

It is, of course, impossible to deny that thus far national power and responsibility have been increasing. The reason national government has assumed such a large role is that in far too many cases state government has been unresponsive to the needs of its citizens. However, it is impractical to conclude that given these circumstances, state governments can *never* be responsive. An equally logical and possible alternative would be a more viable federal system. Centralization of responsibility is not the only answer. In order to strengthen the federal system much needs to be done; the state governments must be reorganized. The executive branch must be carefully restructured and made more efficient. Governors must be given the tools and the authority to do the job. The imbalance of power between state executive branches and state legislative branches must be redressed. Just as in the struggle between national and state government, the power has flowed to the national government, so too in the struggle between the executive and legislative branch, the governor has usurped power that belongs to the legislators.

The chapters in this section discuss and illustrate the problems involved in alleviating the imbalances in the federal system, and, in our opinion, demonstrate the significance of our recommendations. We propose increased state responsibility, not because we sympathize with the John Birchers, but because we believe in a more viable federal system tailored to the needs of modern society.

CHAPTER FOUR

An Attempt to Innovate: The California Federal Legislative Office

The overall performance of the American state legislatures in the twentieth century has not been anywhere near outstanding. Generally speaking, the reasons for this are twofold. First, most state legislatures are severely hampered by outmoded internal operation and outdated constitutional restrictions. Second, the relative influence of state administrations has greatly increased, often at the expense of state legislatures. But in some states, notably the largest and most "progressive" by traditional standards, significant reforms have been made. Most importantly for this discussion, the California Legislature should be considered in the vanguard of legislative progress.

Reform of state legislatures has taken place on many fronts. In some states, elimination of outdated restrictions on the length of legislative sessions and/or on salary schedules are the first order

Source: This essay, which describes the operation and impact of the first office operated by a state legislature in Washington, is adapted from a research paper written by Mr. Stephen B. Andrews, an Eagleton Fellow from 1967–1968. The paper was prepared as part of his assignment in a Seminar in Practical Politics taught by Donald Herzberg and Jess Unruh.

of business for the reformers. In other states, the overhaul of an ancient committee system may seem most important as a first step. Always of primary concern, however, is the area of staffing. The importance of providing legislators with information and technical assistance is reflected in the tremendous upgrading of the staff function in modernized state legislatures.

As a state legislature develops a viable internal decision-making apparatus and frees itself from undue exterior restrictions, it inevitably enhances its potential for significant policy making. And, as with all units of government, the impact and importance of the federal government becomes even more visible. A modern state legislature, with the will and the resources to participate meaningfully in the policy-making process, cannot help but become involved with the federal government. It is in this context—the importance of staffing to meaningful lawmaking and the overall impact of the federal government on the administrative and policy alternatives of the states—that one must see the creation and operation of the California Federal Legislative Office.

The California Federal Legislative Office was established in January 1967, by action of the state legislature's Joint Budget Committee. There was no specific appropriation for the office by the legislature itself, and it remains directly responsible to the Joint Legislative Budget Committee. The activities of the office are coordinated by the legislative analyst's office, a primary staff arm of the legislature. Its annual budget is $50,000, plus some minimal expense account monies. The first director of the office, William Lipman, served for seven years in the California State Office of Planning and before that had been a special assistant for planning in the office of the Assistant Secretary of the Army.

The perceived need for a Federal Legislative Office on the part of those in leadership positions in Sacramento is no doubt more complex than the following discussion might suggest. In large part, the motivation grew out of the overall modern orientation of the California Legislature. The concepts of a "co-equal" and "coordinate policy-making" legislative body have become realities in California. One of the primary reasons for this development can be found in the greatly increased ongoing resources of the legislature (the staff function discussed above).

The importance of staff resources to a modern legislature should not be underestimated. Increased staff is one of the first priorities of those involved in legislative reform. The California

Federal Legislative Office is an extension of the highly developed staff resources of the California Legislature.

The creation of the legislature's Washington office can also be seen in the light of the growing importance of the federal government. If a state legislature expects to maintain a high-level policy-making role, it must be aware of, react to, and, hopefully, influence the federal government. Just as increased staff resources in the state capital enable the legislature to increase its capabilities in relationship to state issues, so logically will increased staff resources on the federal level enable the legislature to deal more effectively with the influence of the national government.

Another factor in the creation of the federal office was undoubtedly the changing political picture in the state. With the election of a Republican governor, the Democratic leadership of the legislature saw the state's only contact in Washington change partisan orientation. One of the basic tenets of a "co-equal" legislature is that it has independent sources of information, and the difference in partisan orientation between the governor and the legislative leadership made the independence of Washington information particularly suspect.

The director of the Federal Legislative Office organizes his activities in a very systematic manner. Basically, he perceives the Washington office as an extension of the research capabilities of the California Legislature. He hopes, in his terms, to provide "alternative inputs" to the state legislative system. His original perceptions of the functions of the office are worth quoting in depth:

> *First,* with respect to Federal legislation now in force, to determine how the State Government can take maximum advantage of Federal financial and technical assistance, with particular emphasis on those steps that may need to be taken by the Legislature to enable the State Government to phase into existing Federal programs.
>
> *Second,* with respect to proposed policies and programs, and to newly enacted legislation where administrative standards have not been finally established, to make known to responsible Federal officials the considered views of the Legislature . . . with the objective of influencing administrative determinations and policy and program design in the State's favor, especially with regard to financial assistance.
>
> *Third,* with respect to the longer-term development of Federal policies and programs . . . to inform the Legislature about

advance planning and evolving Federal policy and program development. . . .
Fourth, with respect to known areas of Legislative inquiry and concern, to provide independently, and on its . . . own initiative, advice and assistance, data, contact with institutions and persons, and other services to support the conduct of Legislative inquiries and research activities.
Fifth, with respect to taking advantage of available Federal programs where no legislative action is required, to continually appraise the degree to which State agencies are making maximum possible use of financial and technical assistance.

Within the broad category of "information services," the Washington office organizes its basic, day-to-day communications with the legislature in Sacramento. Under the heading "general information," the office, on its own initiative, sends a constant stream of potentially useful information to Sacramento. Included here are general items such as newspaper articles, publications, reports of federal agencies, and so on. Once a week a list of the material sent is forwarded to the legislative analyst, the chief minority consultant, and the director of the Office of Research.

In the category of "reply memoranda" the Washington office responds to requests for specific information from committee consultants, the Office of Research, or individual legislators. The Washington office operates in this capacity through the legislative analyst, who coordinates and organizes the requests from the various sources mentioned previously. The reasons for this arrangement grew out of a concern for confidentiality and possible duplication of effort. There developed in the first months of the operation of the office some problems in this area, which resulted in a series of memos from the chairman of the Joint Legislative Committee and from the legislative analyst's office to legislators and staff members concerning the necessity of this requirement for channeling requests.

The third category under this general heading of information services is labeled "information advice letters." Periodically the director will forward reports to Sacramento on information sources available in Washington that may be of use to staff personnel or individual legislators. If at some future date there is need for such information, its availability and existence are already known. An example of this type of service is the "monthly statistical recap," a memorandum sent to Sacramento once a month, listing studies, reports, and data potentially useful to research staffs in the legislature. The first recap, in October 1967, included information on (1) the Congressional Joint Economic Committee study plan for 1967, (2) the new statistical maps on ethnic population, (3) the new census series, (4) the Michigan Manpower Study, and (5) "Aptitude Requirements for 500 Occupations."

The final category under this general heading is termed "federal office memoranda." These memoranda deal with the information on substantive issues gathered through interviews with federal officials, private institutions, and so on. They cover a wide variety of issues of concern to the California Legislature. Following are four areas involving federal office memoranda in May 1967:

1. Inquiry on evolving the substantive character of the concept of "creative federalism," including both a broader view of state–federal issues and the specific activity of task forces established pursuant to Johnson's message to to Congress on "Quality of American Government"
2. Pursuance of both federal and nonfederal activities in the field of social accounting, involving persons at the Twentieth Century Fund, Yale University, and HEW
3. Provision of preliminary information on the Defense Department's "Project Aristotle"
4. Identification for subsequent action of promising areas of inquiry in the area of government science policy

The second broad category of activities performed by the Washington office involves the communication of information relevant to programs being developed in Sacramento. The director receives both general and specific requests from Sacramento. An example of the former would be a request to secure from HEW and other agency people some indication of the kinds of state legislation they would like to see attempted and would be willing to assist in developing through joint research and development activities. Information on more specific legislative issues ranges from an analysis of the effect of proposed legislation on federal administrative agencies to long-term involvement of the Washington office in the development of specific state legislation.

The involvement of the Federal Legislative Office in the development of specific legislation is illustrated by the activities of the office pertaining to the automobile emission standards legislation introduced in the assembly in January 1968.

The first contact between the California Assembly and the Washington office on the emission standards legislation came in December 1967, when the director conferred with various committee consultants on issues involving potential use of the Washington office. As part of this overall contact, he discussed a major package of bills due for hearings before the Assembly Committee on Transportation and Commerce with the committee's consultant.

The bills in question, AB 356 and AB 357, dealt with the problem of air pollution in California. The first bill, AB 356, would have established stricter emission standards on all motor vehicles sold in California starting in 1970. The bill provided strong incentives and sanctions for compliance or noncompliance with new standards. The second bill, AB 357, would have used the state's purchasing power to encourage the private sector to develop a smog free car. The state, by agreeing to buy cars with extremely low emission output (that is, steam engine, electric power, gas turbine, and so on), had hoped to encourage a technological breakthrough in this field. The Federal Legislative Office became involved in the development of this second bill.

The director, being based in Washington, was able to contact such private national organizations as the Ford Foundation's "Resources for the Future, Inc." on the work they were doing in the general field of air pollution control. Other contacts were made with East Coast steam engine developers and those developers testifying before Congress on the potentials of an electric car ("Magnuson Act Hearings"). The director, on the basis of these contacts and conversations with officials in the federal government, drew conclusions and made recommendations to the assembly committee.

On February 25, 1968, the director joined the consultant and two members of the Assembly Transportation Committee in Detroit for two days of conferences on the proposed legislation with representatives of the "Big Three"—General Motors, Ford, and American Motors. Later, on the way to Sacramento for hearings on the bill, the director stopped in Chicago to confer with a prospective witness on the bill. In Sacramento he worked on planning the committee hearings. For the members of the committee, he drew up a series of questions raised by critics of noninternal combustion engines in Detroit and Washington.

After the committee hearings, the director, the committee consultant, and the steam engine developers discussed ways to conduct systems engineering tests to quantify the advantages of unconventional power sources for automobiles. Further meetings were held with the California Highway Patrol on the possibilities of carrying out extensive road tests on the steam engine. Back in Washington, he began exploring unconventional funding sources for conducting the tests with the California Highway Patrol. Again utilizing its Washington base, the Federal Legislative Office could contact private individuals and foundations, as well as elements within the federal government, in exploring reactions and comments on the proposed California legislation.

The fourth and final general classification of services performed by the federal office includes a wide variety of liaison activities. This aspect of the office's services is extremely flexible, and primarily involves the maintenance of ongoing contacts with individuals, agencies, and institutions whose work has present or future implications for California.

The bulk of the federal office's liaison work is directed toward administrative agencies and departments, most importantly Health, Education, and Welfare; Housing and Urban Development; and the Department of Defense. The director attempts to develop contacts that will yield both substantive information of relevance to California and ongoing relationships that can be used by other California officials when they are in Washington.

The coordination of the activities of other California legislative officials when in Washington reflects both the impact of the federal government on state issues and the growing development of periodic contacts between officials representing the two units of government. Recently the Washington office arranged an extensive set of meetings between legislative staff people and senior officials of the Bureau of the Budget, HEW, and other executive departments, as well as congressional staff and policy planners and advisers outside the federal establishment whose work is of interest to the legislature. The California officials (the director of the Assembly Office of Research, committee consultants representing the Assembly Revenue and Taxation, Public Health, Social Welfare, and Industrial Relations Committees, and the legislative assistant of the Assembly Speaker) spent an entire week in Washington. The liaison activities of the federal office also extend to institutions and individuals outside the federal government who are headquartered in Washington. The contacts are often initiated by these sources themselves, for instance, in the form of corporate representatives who are interested in applying their know-how to the state's educational problems. The activities of the federal office during the development of the emission standards legislation also points out the importance of having an ongoing Washington base for the state legislature.

Although the primary importance of the liaison activities of the Federal Legislative Office is probably the information communicated to Sacramento, the value of the reverse should also be noted. The contacts made with federal officials cannot help but make them more aware of the activities and desires of the California Legislature—the body responsible for applying and overseeing much of the federal legislation that pertains to the state. The development of ongoing contacts in this area could well make federal officials more sensitive, and hopefully more responsive to the problems faced by the state legislature as it attempts to develop rational, consistent policies.

An integral part of the liaison activities of the Washington office involves travel for consulting with universities and nonprofit organizations and attending conferences and experimental projects when time or distance considerations preclude attendance by people from Sacramento. The director also travels to Sacramento once every two months for discussions with legislators and staff personnel on their immediate or long-range concerns that potentially involve the Washington office.

A final aspect of the liaison activities of the Federal Legislative Office relates to Congress. Until January 1968, a full year after the office was established, there was little or no contact with "the Hill." The reasons for this are varied, but in part resulted from political sensitivities in both Washington and Sacramento. In a memorandum to the files in January 1968, the director noted that the office was "free to pursue technical discussions with congressional staffers and legislative liaison people in the executive departments."

One result of this orientation has been the development of a reporting service on legislation introduced in the second session of the 90th Congress. The legislature requested a "more comprehensive and rapid transmission of information regarding pending federal legislation," and to this end the Washington office now provides a continuous bill service, and every two weeks sends a summary of the progress of the relevant legislation to the Assembly Office of Research and the Minority Consultant's Office.

In summary, the California Federal Legislative Office performs three major functions. It provides, first of all, service and information to the California Legislature. Although it is a staff arm of the legislature, it does not do in-depth research. Its activities in this area can be seen as providing information and sources of information to those in the legislature who are involved in such research. The information ranges from answers to specific requests from legislative staff people to a bill service and analysis of the progress of legislation in the United States Congress.

The second overall function of the federal office involves liaison activities with the administration, Congress, and private institutions headquartered in Washington. This liaison work yields both immediate information and ongoing contacts that can be used at some future date by other legislative members or staff people, or by the Washington office itself.

Finally, the Washington office performs a representative function for California and, most importantly, for the California Legislature. The value of this function is obvious. The California Legislature must apply and oversee a great deal of federal legislation, and if its views can be made known to those drafting legislation and developing administrative standards, the potentials for conflict and friction can be substantially reduced. The California Federal Legislative Office is an innovation for both state legislatures and for public representation in general. Its creation, operation, and problems are unique in the sense that it is an integral part of a *legislative body*, rather than an administrative or executive one. However, the California Federal Legislative Office cannot be separated from the larger picture of governmental representation on the federal level. Its operation and impact are influenced in the same manner and by the same factors as are other Washington offices, and it must be aware of and sensitive to this broader orientation if it is to fulfill its potential as a Washington representative of the California Legislature.

The development of effective relationships between the Washington office and Congress is perhaps the most troublesome issue facing the federal office. At first glance, close and cordial relationships would seem obvious; the orientation of both parties seems to be legislative, not administrative or executive. The situation, unfortunately, is just the reverse.

The basic reason for lack of contact between the federal office and the California congressional delegation is a conscious avoidance of "the Hill" by the director of the office. At the time of the establishment of the office, such avoidance was eminently reasonable, and in fact, instructions to this effect were apparently included in the original establishment of the office. However, this orientation seems neither necessary nor appropriate in view of subsequent experience.

The original reasons for the avoidance of Capitol Hill were basically political. Several Democratic members of the California delegation saw the establishment of the Federal Legislative Office as a potential front for the intrusion of former Assembly Speaker Jess Unruh into national politics, and in some cases there was strong opposition. This factor was coupled with what can only be called jealousy of congressional prerogatives on the part of several members of the delegation. Some members were afraid that the Federal Legislative Office would tip off state senators and assemblymen on programs, appointments, appropriations, and so on, that congressmen themselves want to announce back home. For these reasons, avoidance of the congressional delegation was a primary consideration in the early operation of the office. The misconceptions concerning the purpose and operation of the office may not have been corrected, but at least the issue was deflated.

As of April 1968 the hostility directed toward the establishment of the federal offices was apparently dispelled, although misconceptions about its activities were still great. In January of 1968 the legislature asked for more rapid and comprehensive information on the impact and chances for passage of bills affecting California interests, and to this end a bill service was established. The Washington office was still reluctant, however, to approach Capitol Hill. The director saw his new mandate as directed toward congressional staff, not toward establishment of contacts with individual members of the California delegation.

There appears to be major advantages of increasing communication between the Federal Legislative Office and the California delegation. Generally speaking, it makes good sense to have as much ongoing contact as possible between the state legisature, which has to react to federal legislation, and the California congressional delegation, which has a voice in its development. Everyone involved is concerned with (1) California, and (2) legislative politics; with this much in common, a greater degree of contact should be highly desirable. The nature of contacts on Capitol Hill could vary considerably, from one-time-only courtesy calls to continuous relationships with individual congressmen.

Under the general heading of public relations arise several

potential and immediate problems for the California Federal
Legislative Office. In the following discussion there are two implicit assumptions: (1) the concept of a federal office for a highly
developed state legislature as in California, is a viable and even
necessary innovation for state legislative politics, and (2) considering the realities of changing political situations, a perpetual
life span for such an innovation is not necessarily assured, no
matter how necessary, useful, or efficient it might appear to be.

The overall awareness of the existence and functions of the
California Federal Legislative Office on the part of the California
congressional delegation and public representatives from California and other states is not nearly as great as it should be. Other
Washington representatives from cities and counties in California
were generally unaware of the existence of the legislative office,
or else they had little or no idea about its purpose or functions.
Similarly, several new members of the California congressional
delegation were also unaware of the existence of the legislative
office.

The difference between the visibility of the governor's representatives and the legislative office is extreme. As an example,
the governor's office often asks for information from the legislative office. Cross-checking on the ultimate destination of this information, it seems that it often goes to individuals or institutions
outside the California circle of representatives. If the legislative
office were better known, contacts could be made directly, with
obvious implications for the prestige of the California legislature.
Knowledge is, in a real sense, influence, and the advantages of
serving as a broker of such knowledge has in this case been dis-
sipated.

A more general reason for an increased public relations
effort on the part of the Federal Legislative Office relates to its
uniqueness among American state legislatures. Assuming it is a
viable innovation, worthy of consideration by other states that
will hopefully reach a similar level of legislative development, it
seems logical that increased publicity concerning the office would
yield positive benefits.

In general, then, increased public relations efforts on the
part of the Washington office seem imperative in order to (1)
inform those who logically should know of the existence of the
office, (2) eliminate some of the misconceptions as to the purposes and activities of the office on the part of the congressional
delegation, California, and the other state and local public repre-

sentatives in Washington, and (3) increase the potential for direct contacts with those seeking information available through the office.

Clearly, the California Federal Legislative Office should perform a more forceful role of self-advocacy. It represents a unique innovation in American state legislatures, and as such its performance deserves as wide an audience as possible.

CHAPTER FIVE

The New Role
of State
and Local Government

Perhaps the most outstanding characteristic of American politics in the 1960s will someday be seen as the emergence of the city as a political issue. To be sure, government has long addressed itself to the separate components of the urban experience—unemployment, deterioration of housing, segregation, crime, disease —but only in this decade have we developed a sense of the effect of all of these forces working together in the modern metropolis.

With this awareness has come an increasing concern with the validity of ideas intended to solve urban problems. Money and manpower alone are not enough. Money and manpower must be invested in the *right* programs, or the result will be cynicism among those people whose taxes pay the bill and frustration among those people whose problems are not being solved.

A general criticism of our present approach is that the domestic programs of the central government over the last thirty years have become so pervasive and so dominant that other problem-solving resources are discouraged and even prevented

Source: Adapted from a talk given by Jess Unruh at a Seminar in Practical Politics, December 7, 1968, at the Eagleton Institute of Politics, Rutgers University, New Brunswick, New Jersey.

from creating and implementing solutions. Much recent federal legislation reveals a lack of confidence that states, and particularly state legislatures, can respond to the needs of their citizens.

The widespread consequences of the ultimate decline of the states and of federal dependency of cities, school districts, and universities should be carefully examined before the process goes much further.

Representative democracy that is reasonably close to the people will have collapsed. The United States Congress will be left as the only effective organ of representative government in the entire country. The only restraint on federal executive power will rest with Congress and the United States Supreme Court. How will the federal government and the political parties function if the states do not perform a checks-and-balances function? What are the implications for the future of democratic government if we cannot make the system work at the state level?

For the most part, the growth of the federal government is *not* due to presidents, bureaucrats, and congressmen plotting ways to seize more power. On the contrary, they seem caught between the pressure to accommodate increased needs, demands, and crises in the population, and the pressure to give meaningfulness and effectiveness to the great diverse muddle of programs that they have established. As a consequence of this, there is little long-range overall thinking and planning about where the country is or should be headed; certainly, very little thought is given to the future of the democratic system of government.

In discussing the future of the states, we are severely handicapped by the traditions of the recent past. Tragically, states' rights have been identified with the rights of some states to maintain two classes of citizenship. Moreover, in recent history, states' rights have been identified with the notion that government at all levels should do very little. These notions, of course, have not disappeared. Americans need to rise above the kind of thinking that identifies the rights of states with the right to do nothing.

The states have declined in considerable part because of their own failures. State government can and must deal more aggressively with urban problems if the urban crisis is to be resolved and if the states and the federal system are to survive.

No one has a full and adequate prescription for what it will take to resolve the urban crisis, though it is reasonably clear that it will take much. In considering this, we should think in terms of coordination, cooperation, and initiative among the units of government, but we should think primarily in terms of *the people and their problems*.

When we approach the problems associated with the urban crisis from the standpoint of *people* in the ghetto, we have reason to question whether or not (quite apart from the future consequences for the federal system of government) the urban crisis can be resolved through federal action. Even if we assume a tenfold increase in federal aid programs, the experience of the past cannot give us confidence that effective results can be secured when the primary initiative rests with the federal government. Many, if not most of the programs that have been derived from federal initiative have contributed to the alienation of the hard-pressed poor.

The federal government seems most successful with programs such as social security and medicare. These are programs that give the most benefit to middle-class or mainstream citizens in time of crisis. The strength of these programs rests in a clean bureaucratic system, with forms and systems, and clients who know something about forms and systems.

The Department of Agriculture has been eminently successful in developing agricultural technology and in providing basic support during periods of low prices, drought, or other contingencies for essentially self-sufficient farmers. But that department has failed to assume *any* responsibility for rural poverty. As a consequence, the rural poor have migrated to the city slums with no preparation for the city government.

So long as the federal government conducts or sets the rules for the programs, there can be no greater coordination or system on the state and local level than there is in Washington, and there is likely to be less. When we are engaged in problems as deep and complicated as those of the poor, be it rural and urban, Negro, Mexican-American, Puerto Ricans, American Indians, Appalachians, or Ozarkians, we need an approach which will enable, encourage, and reward with a feeling of identification with states and local communities. The federal bureaucracy can never produce this needed sense of community.

We also need a system that will give the poor an opportunity to identify with this system of government. Despite the scandals and swindles connected with the old city political machines, they did provide the European immigrants with the feeling that governmental officials cared about their needs and welfare. The labor unions also provided some of this. Neither city government nor the labor unions have been serving this purpose in the last thirty years, partly because many of the old cities have become predominantly ghettos, and partly because city government and labor unions have become middle class and professionalized.

To this we must add the observation that the urban public school systems went through a period of ignoring their primary mission of providing *equal* educational opportunities for all children. They, like most other institutions, did a far better job for the European immigrants and have done a pathetically poor job for blacks and other contemporary minorities.

Except for a very few of the larger states (including California), state government has not been responsive to the needs associated with the urban crisis and rural poverty. The states have declined in considerable part because of their own failures. Yet state governments can and must deal more aggressively with these problems if the crisis is to be resolved and if the states and the federal system are to survive.

State government, within the present structure of government, still has the power to assume an effective initiative. Indeed it must, *because* of its unique role in the structure of government.

Although the problems of the poor are designated city problems because they occur in the central or core cities, they must be recognized as problems of an entire area. In California, for example, the institutional response to city problems has been restricted and fragmented because the scope of these problems exceeds the ability of local governmental institutions to respond.

In part the limitations on the institutions of local government date back to the first two decades of this century, to the Lincoln-Roosevelt League and to reform pressures under Hiram Johnson. As part of a general reaction to corrupt political machines, the institutions of local government became almost parliamentary in form. Thus, the general laws of California provide, as do the laws of most states, for cities and counties to be governed by city councils or boards of supervisors, composed of part-time elected officials, who have both legislative and executive responsibilities. Under these provisions of the general state law, a mayor is simply the presiding officer of a five-member city council, as is the chairman of the county board of supervisors.

The major cities and counties in California are governed under the terms of their own specific charters and have much greater authority than the smaller cities organized under general state law. City and county charters, however, mirror the underlying attitude of our general state law, which places principal executive authority in the city council and board of supervisors rather than in a strong executive. Most city charters do not even provide for a separately elected mayor. The City Charter of Los Angeles, an exception to this generalization, provides for fifteen city councilmen to be elected from districts within the city. The mayor is elected separately by a citywide vote but he has few real executive powers. The powers that he does have, he must share with the city council, and with a vast number of largely independent administrative boards and commissions.

In addition to the fact that there is no strong executive within California's major cities, it must be noted that existing programs aimed at the urban poor are programs over which city officials, either city councils or mayors, have little direct control. For example:

Welfare is administered by the county. There is no city participation.

Education is administered by school districts. These districts are separately governed and completely independent of city government.

Health, in all but a very few cases, is administered by county health departments which are responsible for insuring that living conditions conform to minimum standards of health. Other aspects of health care are taken care of by federal, state, and county agencies. There is no city participation.

Employment and retraining programs are handled by the state department of employment. Again, there is no city participation.

Redevelopment and Urban Renewal programs are administered by autonomous redevelopment agencies over which the city council has no direct control.

Housing, which is publicly assisted in California, is administered by local housing authorities. Again, such an authority is a quasi-independent agency over which city government has little control.

The point to be made here is that California's cities are not now, and never have been, directly responsible for most of the programs that are directed at problems of urban poverty and slum life. It is unrealistic to expect established local institutional patterns, or the values held by the people of different localities that support these patterns, to change suddenly and assume vast new responsibilities. Rather than castigating an institutional structure fifty years in the making, Americans should seek the answer to this key question: What level of government has comprehensive jurisdiction and legal authority enough, and simultaneously has sufficient sophistication, detailed information, and responsiveness to coordinate a complete attack upon the problems of urban poverty areas?

The state has obvious powers and opportunities that cities and counties do not have. State government has the power to encourage, guide, and prod local government to do more, to do it more effectively, and to do it in keeping with the conditions of local regions.

In considering the need for initiative and leadership from state government, Americans should keep in mind that we still have a federal system. Many programs, even those initiated by Congress, are administered or implemented by the states. Although the states may finally be buried by the urban crisis, they will not die easily and certainly not rapidly enough to resolve the current crisis.

If state government, and especially legislatures, will face up to the needs of the people, more initiative can come from state and local government. This, of course, depends in part on the people. Are the people able and willing to permit state and local government the revenues that are needed, and do governors and legislators have the courage to ask them? These are the kinds of issues that confront governors, legislatures, and voters.

The interest of the cities in solving their problems is directly associated with the more effective operation of state legislatures. This is not just a matter of questioning why the state does not understand the cities' needs, but also a matter of realizing that the legislature itself must be *equipped* to understand the problems of the cities and must go through the difficult problem of weighing these against other needs and interests.

The legislature also has both the right and the obligation to ask whether or not the programs supported by state revenues are effective. If they are not, and if there is a job that vitally needs to be done, it is the obligation of the legislature to suggest constructive alternatives. If representative democracy has any meaning, it is that legislators and city councilmen, and even congressmen, should be closer to the people than executives and administrators. The alternatives initiated by a legislature are likely to be those closer and more meaningful to the people. Pouring additional revenue into state and local government is not sufficient. Government institutions need to be strengthened. Americans need to develop a system of state government that is suitable to the problems of the era.

The cities are the "creatures" of the state. To broaden the powers and the opportunities of these units to deal with the problems associated with the urban crisis depends upon state action, especially on legislative action. A legislature that prevents a city from raising its own revenues to meet current problems can certainly expect the city to step up its efforts to get federal revenue. This kind of activity also has the effect of lowering the stature of the city's legislative delegation.

Obviously, cities and other units of local government must be given the autonomy they need to cope with their problems and conduct their own programs. More positively, state government should reward, encourage, prod, and promote such initiative. At the same time, Americans should keep in mind that many cities and counties are not meaningful units of government.

Since all such units are created by state statute or, in some cases, by state constitutions, the meaningful organization and consolidation of local units of government depend on state action.

There has not yet been any study that has thought through in any systematic way, the range or the focus of action that state government can take concerning the problems associated with the urban crisis. Obviously, state statutes need to be reviewed to determine whether and how the poor *are* penalized, for the poor are penalized in diverse and devious ways (for example, the interest rates permitted on short-term, high-risk loans; the tax system, including the loopholes permitted to people who have the ability or the resources to locate the holes; statutes that protect the seller but fail to provide any protection for the consumer; welfare systems that discourage the poor from seeking any form of gainful employment; and juvenile and criminal codes that reasonably protect those who can afford legal services but penalize those who go into court with inadequate legal representation).

The penal institutions, including the so-called juvenile correctional institutions, operate primarily as schools of crime. Those who take the course come out better schooled in how to be a criminal and even more alienated from the orthodox society. This is a complex issue with no ready solution but it is clearly a responsibility of state government, which operates the major sector of the penal system in the country.

While we may not be optimistic that the primary initiative for solving the current crisis *will* come from state government, it is a possibility. The reapportionment of state legislatures, combined with the impact of the crisis, is pushing some state governments toward a realistic confrontation with urban problems.

If the states are to act meaningfully on the current crisis, they must rapidly reverse a trend of fifty years. Governors and agency administrators must change their traditional habits of "thinking small." Legislatures and governors must force state programs to coordinate effectively on the local level and to relate meaningfully to the people.

If the states are to become a viable force, they must think beyond minimal federal standards. Many states should venture, experiment, and set the pace for the rest of the country. The states should exert counterpressure on the federal government to organize itself. To accomplish this, state legislatures will have to be rapidly revitalized.

Obviously, and generally, the *status and authority* of the legislative institution and its role in resolving the problems associated with the urban crisis should be accepted, recognized, and supported by the legislators themselves, the civic leadership, the mass media, and the general public. We know that state legislatures have not in the past served as effectively as they should have as forums for airing the problems of blacks and other minorities. The role of large cities, once served in sociopolitical assimilation, is being met increasingly ineffectively, largely because of the altered composition of the population within the boundaries of the old cities. Thus, state legislatures should be developed and recognized as a meeting place, as a place of negotiation, and as a place for developing understanding among suburbanites and city dwellers, among socioeconomic classes, and among racial and ethnic groups.

The public is not likely to have confidence in its political system if the system is remotely centralized in Washington with bureaucratic blocks between public and program, and between public and policy makers. If public confidence in government depends upon confidence in Washington, it is likely to center on a very transitional confidence in the personality of one man—the President. It is demonstrably dangerous to settle for such a system. The alternative is clearly that of restoring confidence in state and local government. This can only happen if and when state and local governments begin to take action more effectively.

CHAPTER SIX

The State
and the Community:
The Ghetto

It is frequently suggested that the United States adheres, or should adhere, to a doctrine of "one-man, one-vote." Despite the existence of this doctrine, minority groups, often grouped in ghetto areas, are underrepresented in American governmental institutions. This is particularly true in the state legislatures. These representative bodies must be creative enough to recognize this underrepresentation and to respond to it in order to lessen the alienation of black and other minority citizens from the traditional political institutions. The state legislatures are the key to rectifying this inequality. However, before we can detail some suggestions toward this end we should document the problem.

As late as May 1968 the U.S. Commission on Civil Rights, in a study of southern Negro political participation since the passage of the Voting Rights Act of 1965, wrote that despite recent civil rights legislation, "many new barriers to full and equal

Source: Prepared by Donald G. Herzberg, Jess Unruh, and Alan S. Chartock especially for this volume.

political participation have arisen. . . ." [1] The commission cited
the practices of "diluting the votes of Negroes, preventing Negroes
from becoming candidates, discriminating against Negro regis-
trants and poll watchers, and discriminating against Negroes in
the appointment of election officials."

Of course, these abuses are also practiced outside of the
South. The President's National Commission on Registration and
Voting Participation wrote in 1963 that: "Many people are discouraged, if not barred outright, by complicated and inaccessible
registration." [2]

As a result of the frustrations of a discriminatory society,
the refusal of many members of minority groups to deal through
"legitimate" established political channels has now been demonstrated. G. Franklyn Edwards has pointed to the "manifest desire
of Negroes to maintain social distance from whites in community
relations as a result of their perception of the adverse use of
power by whites."

The inability and refusal of many minority group members
to utilize the political and the more confined legislative process
to achieve fulfillment may be attributed to a number of variables.
One such variable has been the resistance of American society
to upgrade educational standards in ghetto and minority areas.
This refusal has perpetuated a vicious circle in which the political
role of the black man in America has been severely weakened.
As a result of the refusal to close the education gap, the verbal
and communicative abilities of minority groups have suffered.
The latter abilities are, of course, two essential ingredients for
successful participation in the American political system.

Daniel Moynihan succinctly pinpointed the problem when
he suggested that the racist "virus" in the American blood stream
vitally affects us all. He states that:

> Individually, Negro Americans reach the highest peaks of
> achievement. But collectively, in the spectrum of American
> ethnic and religious and regional groups, where some get plenty
> and some get more, where some send eighty percent of their

[1] U.S. Commission on Civil Rights, *Political Participation: A Study
of the Participation by Negroes in the Electoral Processes in 10 Southern States since Passage of the Voting Rights Act of 1965* (Washington, D.C.: Government Printing Office, 1968), p. iii.
[2] *Report of President's National Commission on Registration and
Voting Participation* (Washington, D.C.: Government Printing Office,
November, 1963).

children to college and others pull them out of school at the 8th grade, Negroes are among the weakest.[3]

Existing studies strongly suggest that by making quality education inaccessible to the black man, he has been deprived in a number of ways. As David B. Ryckman has pointed out: "Language studies on social class generally have found that children from lower social and economic groups are deficient in language skills, from the early development of speech sounds to higher levels of abstract usage." [4]

The implications of this educational impairment in terms of social and political participation, are substantial. According to Truman Temple, "Native-born Negroes either from urban ghettos or southern rural areas have the most conspicuous problem. In the restrained phrases of one professional in linguistics, they are often denied employment because of speech patterns that disqualify them or awaken negative stereotypes in the minds of listeners." [5]

The political participation of ghetto residents is likewise limited by inadequate primary and secondary education. Increasing evidence points to a correlation between political attitudes and education. The unwillingness of American society to provide and insist on first-class education for black and other minority citizens has been partially responsible for a chauvinistic political system. The U.S. Commission on Civil Rights has written that as late as 1968, "Negroes still are excluded from the affairs of many state and local party organizations or feel unwelcome. . . ." They further state that: "Neither the Democratic or Republican national party organization has taken adequate steps to deal with this problem."

Instead of seeking to open the political process to the black man, Americans have often done just the opposite. The President's Commission on Registration and Voting Participation has pointed to the literacy test as one such device. The commission

[3] Daniel Patrick Moynihan, "The Negro Family: The Case for National Action," in Lee Rainwater and William L. Yancy, eds., *The Moynihan Report and the Politics of Controversy* (Cambridge: M.I.T. Press, 1967), p. 43.

[4] David B. Ryckman, "A Comparison of Information Processing Abilities of Middle and Lower Class Negro Kindergarten Boys," in *Exceptional Children*, Vol. 33, No. 8 (April 1967), pp. 545–552.

[5] Truman R. Temple, "Program for Overcoming the Handicap of Dialect," *New Republic*, Vol. 156 (March 25, 1967), pp. 11–12.

has recommended that literacy tests should not be required for voting. According to the commission, "Racial discrimination by means of unfair administration of literacy tests is a perversion of the democratic process. The institution of the literacy test deprives those most outside the political process of access to it. Other practices, such as high filing fees and difficult petition standards, also keep the economically and educationally deprived from running for office."

This is substantiated by William Keefe and Morris Ogul, who find that, "By and large, Negroes have not won as much from politics as their numbers warrant. . . . Discrimination diminishes their power. This is especially true in the holding of elective offices." [6] Keefe writes that Negro underrepresentation often occurs because "a densely populated Negro community is likely to be compressed into one, two, or a few legislative districts. . . ." He concludes, "Negro legislators, it is safe to say, are produced by an irreducible number of Negro districts." [7] There are, of course, exceptions to this, such as San Francisco, where an outstanding Negro Assemblyman consistently wins a district with a 25 percent or less black constituency.

Often, black and other minority groups are seriously underrepresented in a more subtle manner. In districts where blacks and the poor constitute a minority, they are underrepresented by legislators with nonblack perspectives. Because of the lack of identification between the representative and minority constituent, a feeling of frustration often results. Lewis Dexter reports that: "A Congressman hears most often from those who agree with him." According to Dexter, "A Congressman's relationship with his district tends to be maintained through a group who have since then worked closely with him. . . . Some men automatically interpret what they hear to support their viewpoints." [8] Minority groups, different from their representatives, can hardly expect to find their interests represented by a man with an entirely different world view.

Many white institutions cannot be utilized by the black man

[6] William J. Keefe and Morris S. Ogul, *The American Legislative Process: Congress and the States*, 2d edition. (Englewood Cliffs, N.J.: Prentice-Hall, Inc., 1968), p. 128.

[7] Keefe and Ogul, *The American Legislative Process*, p. 128.

[8] Lewis Anthony Dexter, "The Representative and His District," in Robert L. Peabody and Nelson W. Polsby, eds., *New Perspectives on the House of Representatives* (Skokie, Ill.: Rand McNally and Company, 1963), p. 11.

with equal success. This is particularly true of governmental institutions. While the black and other minority communities may have achieved reform in some policy areas, such as educational reforms and in community mental health, there has been little similar work in the reform of governmental institutions.

If verbal and educational handicaps have placed the black man in an inferior status in the social system, the same variables have been responsible for an underrepresentation in the political institutions. Prevailing theories of representative government are based on the ability of the constituent to communicate and verbalize his needs and aspirations to his representatives. According to these theories, the legislator embodies the needs of his constituency into proposed public policy.

The main methods of communication between the legislator and his district are telephone, face-to-face meetings, public forums, and written communication. Since these communication forms are based on verbal and educational foundations, the more verbal and learned a constituent is, the larger the share of the representative's time he commands.

The existent power structure must recognize that it may further its own rational self-interest by recruiting black and other minority groups into the system and by assigning a far greater share of the product of society to them. It has been suggested that the vast urban patterns of housing, schooling, employment, and public services must be reshaped if equal opportunity is to be realized in fact as well as in principle. If this is done, an increased sense of political efficacy will be constituted in all citizens and it is hoped that in such a way the society can be far more productive and beneficial to all of its participants.

There is a justifiable fear on the part of the critics of those who advocate reform of the existing system, that such reform is aimed at cooptation rather than social change. Nevertheless, to argue thusly is to give credence to the theory that all piecemeal institutional and social change is irrelevant, social security, medicare, and public education notwithstanding.

Within the ghetto areas, spokesmen for the black communities have arisen representing differing shades of opinion that range from integration to separation, and that sometimes have considerably overlapping boundaries. As we have already suggested, the American political system is structured in such a way as to respond to those persons from any community who have verbal communicative, as well as economic assets. The danger is that our political leadership has no knowledge of where else to turn. The destructive elements who do not wish to see increased participation by minority groups in the framework of the present political process, naturally respond to any verbal element within the minority community that will verify their racist theories and will cite them as examples of black aspirations. American politicians have the delicate twofold task in front of them of encouraging positive minority leadership, on the one hand, and of discovering who and what are representative of minority aspirations and demands on the other. It should be noted that the two are not antithetical.

Up to this point, we have attempted to document the built-in biases against blacks and minorities implicit in the American political system and particularly its representative bodies. The basic assumption we make is that the system must continually rejuvenate itself and adhere to the widely accepted creed of American democracy known as "equality of opportunity."

It is our proposal that American legislatures, which are themselves now going through an introspective period, extend and change the concept of representative democracy. This would involve the recognition that underrepresented ghetto residents have political aspirations and demands that can be identified and embodied into proposed legislation. The legislature must recognize that these demands cannot always be verbalized in the traditional manner, and do not have traditional types of support —much like many consumer issues—and must, therefore, be overrepresented by individual legislation or party action.

Policymakers in the state legislature must react creatively. If legislators rely on the traditional verbal, literate tools of the lawyer, we will not be able to meet the challenge. The legislature must rely heavily on the social science methods and techniques that have been developed in the colleges and universities. Now, because of the critical juncture in American history, we must develop communication links between the business world, the university, and the legislature, which will allow the new technology to be applied in the ghetto area. Here, dividends on the investment in state university research, as well as teaching, can be demonstrated to the legislator who has previously balked at such expenditures. The state legislature has the dual task of providing immediate reaction to rational minority group demands, as well as providing for effective long-range planning. This may well be one realistic way of avoiding having those groups take to the street in support of their demands.

For this reason, we make the following recommendations:

1. The legislature, as a whole, should create a research staff charged with research into areas where minorities live in crowded and unsatisfactory conditions.
2. This staff should utilize professional consultation from each of the existing disciplines with careful cross-pollinization.
3. It should be the job of the staff to identify needs and aspirations of the community, avoiding the present pitfalls of relying exclusively on verbal representations, and ignoring those who lack verbal ability.
4. This unit should be headed by persons recognizing the basic premise of underrepresentation of black and other minority groups. It should have an advisory board composed mainly of minority group members and ensure against cooptation.
5. The unit should remain in constant contact with the constructive minority leadership attempting to improve on a basically unequal system of allocating resources.
6. The unit should utilize innovative and established social science techniques for measuring the demands of the community.
7. These techniques should include some kind of consistent polling of ghetto residents for opinions concerning the formulation of new public policy.
8. A system of priorities should be developed to ensure proper use of scarce resources.

Instead of having an administration program reacted to by a verbal minority, alternatives would be offered by the legislative unit to stratified probability samples. Such issues as varieties of school decentralization, methods of operating welfare programs, crime in the streets, and the question of new businesses for ghetto residents would be presented in an understandable manner to the ghetto sample by persons from the ghetto, who have some ongoing rapport with that community.

The attractive feature of this plan is that individuals who up to now have not come forth to express themselves because of verbal limitations, lack of faith in the system, and lack of knowledge concerning the institution would be approached for the first time, and consistently thenceforth. When and if public policy were actually effectuated as a result of this solicitation, a sense of political participation might well result.

The new procedures would have to be carefully thought out

in the same way as have new educational and intelligence tests for ghetto residents. Nevertheless, social scientists, in utilizing polling techniques, no matter how innovative, still have to rely on communicative and verbal skills.

We therefore recommend the following:

9. New units of analysis dealing with the music, art, and communication forms of the ghetto should be utilized.

   The staff unit should employ sociologists and cultural anthropologists in this area. By looking to art and music forms, it may be possible to ferret out ideas embodied in these media. By looking to art, music, and drama, as well as literary forms, such evident projections as folk music, soul music, rock form, and church music could provide insights and intelligence for the legislature, and might well provide a new set of incentives as well. State art commissions, for example, might well turn their major attention on these areas, much as the WPA Theater group did in the Depression.

10. Small group theory and practice should be utilized in analyzing the political aspirations and goals of the ghetto residents.

    The legislative staff unit might analyze existing communication forms in the ghetto ("stoop to stoop" conversation, gangs, and schools) for establishing priorities and needs, and respond appropriately.

11. It should be the responsibility of the ghetto unit to transmit the acquired information to the legislators who employ them, in such a way that the information does not become desk fodder.

12. Devices such as a short concise newsletter, as well as frequent seminars, bringing Negro leaders to the legislature, should be employed.

    These recommendations mean pointing up the political saliency of findings to legislators concerned with reelection, as well as with the good of state, city, and community.

13. Members of the legislature should be encouraged to frequently confront the problems of the ghetto by spending time there.

14. The legislature should hold full meetings in different ghetto areas. This would help demonstrate the accessibility and concern of the legislature for the ghetto

residents.[9] Even though visible positive results of such meetings have often been indiscernible, the mere evidence of being willing to listen assuredly has a positive underlying effect.

15. A state-by-state study of discriminatory election practices should be undertaken. Such practices as inaccessible polling places, difficult registration procedures, and confining election hours should be discontinued and replaced by more attractive procedures.

A strengthening of the state-by-state electoral and political processes is necessary throughout the country. The way in which leadership evolves in all communities is important. The chance of getting the poor, the black, and the Puerto Rican into the state legislature, where he can express the aspirations of his community, is most important. The recruitment of black and minority groups into the programs relating to participation within the legislative process is as important as recruitment programs that are now operational in university recruitment and poverty programs. By definition, the minority is often unable to be represented in the state legislature. Other expanded forms of legislative representation must be developed. The need is urgent and the staff agencies described in the preceding should be implemented immediately.

A further possibility, deserving of study, is to give those minority legislators who do get elected more staff in order to heighten their decisional impact.

[9] The authors wish to thank Professor Ross Baker of Rutgers University for this suggestion.

CHAPTER SEVEN

The Governor
and the Legislature:
Budgetary and Fiscal Review

American state legislatures must exercise independent judgment in the budget-making process. There is more than a little irony in the fact that such a premise has to be stated at all. It has been axiomatic in the American political system for generations that the executive prepares a budget representing *his* policy priorities and that the legislature compares this document with *its* view of policy priorities, and approves or disapproves the budget accordingly. Since only the legislature can appropriate money to implement policy objectives, and since it is supposed to be acting for the people, its appropriative power ought to prevail.

All those close to state government know that in practice, however, textbook definitions of coordinate government are often, unfortunately, not applicable. The reasons for executive dominance in the budgetary process are obvious. Most governors have trained professional staffs who have ready and private access to executive departments. State legislatures are in session only biennially or for a fraction of each year, while the governor and

Source: Adapted from a speech given by Donald G. Herzberg at the National Conference of the Council of State Governments, 16th Annual Meeting, Honolulu, Hawaii, August 19–23, 1963.

his budget bureau are on the job every day. During legislative sessions the time available to individual legislators and to appropriations committees for budget considerations is severely limited. Moreover, when there is time legislators often find to their chagrin that the complexity of modern government is such that they simply do not know the right questions to ask.

Genuine budget review and fiscal analysis often does not take place. This is because the job of being a legislator is usually a part-time occupation (Chapter Eight deals with the problem of part-time legislators). The governor's budget is either rubber-stamped, or worse, spurious controversies rage over peripheral issues. Often, all that is accomplished is that the budget is cut by a fraction of 1 percent. This kind of legislative budget cutting simply demonstrates to the budget professionals and other interested spectators that legislative expertise is indeed lacking.

What can state legislatures do to improve or reestablish their coordinate position vis-à-vis the executive branch? Forty-one states have sought to answer this pressing question by arranging for some method of legislative budget review. There has been general recognition that professional staff assistance is a prerequisite to the legislature's independent, meaningful, and relevant judgment on appropriations.

An effective legislative fiscal review agency is organized under a statute that specifically sets forth the legislative intent in establishing the agency. Usually this intent is summarized in the assignment of duties to the agency director. As an example of a good law serving this purpose, the following is a synopsis of the legislation establishing the Office of the Legislative Budget and Finance Director in the state of New Jersey.

In Chapter 267 of the Laws of 1954, the director is charged with responsibility for (1) collecting and assembling information relating to the fiscal affairs of the state, for the use of the Joint Appropriations Committee of the legislature in formulating its annual proposals as to amounts to be appropriated for the support of the state government and for other purposes. He examines all requests for appropriations made by the divisions and subdivisions of the principal department of the executive branch of the state government and attends hearings held thereon as may be necessary to obtain complete information as to the subject matter thereof. All budget requests and revenue estimates made by each spending agency of the state are filed with the legislative budget and finance director simultaneously with the filing thereof in the division of budget and accounting of the executive department.

The director is further charged with responsibility for (2) investigating for truth, fairness, and correctness of all claims against the state for payment of which appropriations are to be requested; (3) acting as secretary to the chairman of the Joint Appropriations Committee, attending each session of the full committee and of its various subcommittees; (4) approving all transfers of appropriated funds from one state agency to another or from one line item to another within a state agency; (5) certifying to the governor all expenditures by the legislature, its committees, joint committees, and legislative commissions, thus ensuring that all budget requests by the legislative branch emanate from the same agency; and (6) performing such other duties and collecting such other factual information as the legislature may require to be performed and collected.

In Chapter 27 of the Laws of 1962, the legislative budget and finance director in New Jersey received the additional duty of reviewing and examining for accuracy all fiscal notes accompanying bills that would affect revenues or expenditures. By this legislation, fiscal notes are prepared for legislative fiscal agency review by the executive branch in order to provide an accurate dollar estimate of the amount by which state revenues would be increased or the amount of the appropriation required to meet the purpose of a given bill.

In 1956, Colorado's Joint Budget Committee hired a professional staff that was given the following basic responsibilities: (1) to study the management, operations, programs, and fiscal needs of the agencies and institutions of Colorado state government; (2) to hold hearings as required and to review the executive budget and the budget requests of each state agency and institution, including proposals for construction of capital improvements, and to make appropriation recommendations to the House Appropriations and Senate Finance Committees; (3) to make estimates of revenue from existing and proposed taxes and to make its staff facilities available, upon request, to the finance committees of either house for the development and analysis of proposed revenue measures; and (4) to study and periodically review the state's fund structure, financial condition, fiscal organization, and its budgeting, accounting, reporting, personnel, and purchasing procedures.

Oregon provides a third and final example of an individual state's approach to the question of defining staff responsibilities. The position of legislative fiscal officer was established in 1959 with the powers to: (1) ascertain facts and make recommendations to the legislative assembly concerning the governor's budget report; (2) ascertain facts and make estimates concerning state revenues and expenditures; (3) ascertain facts and make recommendations concerning the fiscal implications of the organization and functions of the state and its agencies; (4) ascertain facts and make recommendations on such other matters as may be provided for by joint or concurrent resolution; (5) furnish such assistance in the performance of their duties as is requested by the Emergency Board, the Joint Ways and Means Committee, the House Taxation Committee, the Senate Taxation Committee and other legislative standing and interim committees and members of the legislative assembly.

The legislative intent of New Jersey, Colorado, and Oregon cannot be clearer. But once a state legislature has decided upon and codified what it wants a professional staff to do in the way of budget review and fiscal analysis, it must then decide who the staff shall be. The best conceived fiscal review agency cannot fulfill its aims if it is not staffed by capable people. What are the characteristics of a good staff director or member?

First, a staff director can be judged by the quality of the staff he chooses, but this is perhaps begging the question. A good staff director has judgment mature enough to realize the limitations of his office as it operates within the law which established it. It is not a second division of budget and accounting. He does not have the resources to match the executive branch estimate for estimate and analysis for analysis. This is not really his function in any case. His function is rather an educative one, to supply to the legislature explanatory information making clear in laymen's terms the mysteries of the administration budget. Being responsible to the legislature and not being committed to the administration's program, he may point out possible effects of an administration proposal, available alternatives, or weaknesses in the administration's reasoning. What may ensue, then, is a dialogue of rational adjustment.

Another invaluable service a good staff director can perform is to provide a realistic appraisal of which part of a given year's budget is negotiable, since a very large part of it is not negotiable. Members of appropriations committees are annually surprised to find that previous legislatures have already committed by statute large portions of the present budget. Thus many budgetary increases are obligatory. Many improvements, such as in capital expenditures to accommodate a rapidly rising population, are virtually mandatory responses to changing conditions that no one can control. The room for maneuver may be so minimal, in fact, that legitimate differences of opinion may exist only on ways to tax for new revenues, not on whether new revenue is needed.

This brings us to the planning function of an effective legislative fiscal review agency. Again, this function dictates to an appreciable degree the kinds of skills needed by a staff. The 1963 *Report of the Committee on Organization of Legislative Services of the National Legislative Conference* did well to differentiate between budget review and fiscal analysis. Budget review, the report said, is "the process of examining proposed expenditures in order to make appropriations for the immediate future." Fiscal analysis, on the other hand, is "the process of obtaining and examining long-term data in order to develop and maintain a sound fiscal program." The key distinction is immediate review versus long-term analysis.

What are the needs of the future? What are the probable future consequences of a given fiscal program? Is only the governor to have a fiscal program? In this area, the legislative fiscal review agency has a truly creative role to play. By forecasting the expanding need for state services, the impact of federal policy on state spending policy, and fluctuating economic changes that influence state revenues, the agency can move the legislature into the fiscal policy-making process well enough in advance to make it an equal partner. Here there is considerable room for negotiation. The alternative is an unplanned, year-to-year fiscal program that tends to move from crisis to crisis.

The legislature might even find that it wants to spend more in certain areas than the governor. State legislatures have acted in recent years as though the only way constituents may be convinced of their sense of legislative responsibility is for them to cut administration budgets. Somewhere in the legislative mind there lurks the fear that taxers and spenders do not get reelected.

The simple fact is, however, that "taxing executives" have fared rather well in the political battle for survival. But a motto of "tax, spend, and elect" is too simple to tell the whole story of executive success in the past thirty years. The further observation is necessary that there was a lack of imaginative legislative leadership available to offer alternatives.

Quite apart from grandiose designs, there is the imminent and practical question of whether the Trenton State Hospital needs a new roof next year, or whether the University of California campus at Riverside needs a new garbage disposal unit for its cafeteria. The administration budget may not provide for these items because someone in the budget bureau did not agree with the urgency of the hospital or university request. The legislature, advised by its fiscal review agency through the Joint Appropriations Committee, might decide that these items will be in the New Jersey and California budgets next year.

In order to know about needed new roofs or garbage disposal units, however, staff members or legislators must visit or otherwise be familiar with local state agencies. Once their needs and problems are known, and if these are being ignored or overlooked by the administration, the legislature might exercise its political responsibility for remedying them. The point is that the legislature is not depending on the administration as its sole source of information and that it has the means to make independent judgments. One cannot overestimate the importance to the legislature of the independent information.

An effective legislative fiscal review agency will have a minimum staff of perhaps six people—a director and five professionals. Not every state legislature can have a large staff, as does California, but their staffs can do essentially the same thing. The staff is organized functionally. There is a director and assistant director (in some cases titled legislative analyst and assistant legislative analyst), a professional in charge of fiscal analysis or research, and two analysts capable of specialized functions (for example, an engineer for capital budget examination or an accountant to pay the necessary attention to executive agency financial statements). All, however, are basically generalists concerned primarily with an agency's processes and programs. Most should have a master's degree in public or business administration. The director especially should have particularly sensitive "political antennae." He must make it clear that he cannot be "used" politically, but he must be aware of the legislature's political problems and of its personalities, moods, and purposes. Reporting on administration nonfulfillment of legislative intent is, after all, one of his most important duties.

The way a staff actually reports to the legislative committee or commission for which it works is worthy of attention. In Texas the staff of the legislative budget board actually prepares a budget and appropriation bill for presentation to the legislature. In California, analysis of the executive budget bill takes the form of a bulky document organized according to items in the budget bill and is cross-referenced to the budget bill by item and by page number. Every item has a recommendation. Typical wording of an analyst's discussion of two recent administration requests in California is:

> The amount budgeted would appear to be a reasonable reflection of the legislature's intent in establishing this program last year and we recommend approval subject to a more adequate presentation of needs and program referred to above.

and

> The operation of the state disaster service now stands at the crossroads. We believe it has reached a point where the legislature must make a decision as to the direction such an organization should take in the future.

The recommendations of a fiscal review staff need not be made in the form of a budget document as in Texas, or an analysis of the executive budget bill as in California. But the recommendations should not be entirely oral or perfunctory in character either, and should be available to appropriations committees well in advance of their public and executive session hearings. Staff attendance at hearings or committee meetings, for the purpose of answering legislators' questions on recommendations, is mandatory.

Lest one think that a legislative fiscal review agency necessarily operates in competition with the budget bureau, let it be said that an effective legislative fiscal staff operates in close cooperation with the administration. This is part of the "dialogue of rational adjustment" discussed earlier.

It is true that many governors oppose the creation of a legislative fiscal staff because, from their point of view, it would (1) encroach upon their executive prerogative and diminish their personal power, (2) constitute recognition of the inadequacy of the executive budget, or (3) threaten duplication of the budget function with resulting waste. Yet the only instances in which such a budget staff has denied the governor full use of the budget as a managerial tool are those where the governor has ignored the budget function and left the initiative to the legislature. A vacuum has thus been filled. In states where strong executive budget offices have been established first, it is unlikely that legislative budget analysts will gain primacy in the budgetary process.

Cooperation may be informal or formal. Whether the legislative staff director attends an executive budget hearing by invitation or by right of law, all concerned recognize he is there doing his job. In Iowa, for example, the legislative fiscal director of the Budget and Financial Control Committee attends all budget hearings and may make whatever inquiries he thinks necessary for complete information. In Illinois and Maine, the legislative budget staffs examine all executive agency requests as they are submitted. By constitutional stipulation in New York, executive departments submit duplicate copies of their budget estimates to the legislative finance committees.

A legislative staff director does well to remember that some of his best information is developed by the courtesy of the budget bureau and not by his legal authority. This is especially true of program (long-term) analysis as differentiated from immediate budget review. As legislative fiscal review agencies turn increasingly toward data processing as an instrument of program analysis, they will depend on raw data which can be supplied only by executive departments through the budget bureau.

Since today most states have legislative budget staffs (forty-one states), some attention should be given to typical shortcomings of staffs already in existence. Most common among these shortcomings is a staff, sometimes through no fault of its own, which is neutralized by the political constituency of the legislature and the governor's party. It might work very hard, for example, when both houses of the legislature are of a different party than the governor. When one or both legislative houses are of the governor's party, however, the legislative staff might either be encouraged to or not allowed to embarrass him. Second there is a tendency in some states to pay off political debts by giving staff jobs to persons, regardless of their professional competence, and legislative leaders become loathe to dismiss an incompetent employee. Third, there is a predilection in some fiscal staff quarters to sit back and let the budget bureau do its work. This is particularly easy in states where the budget bureau is good, and has integrity and a good reputation.

What are the benefits that accrue from the activities of a legislative budget staff when it really does its job? Obviously, an independent review body encourages executive budget analysts to exercise greater care in the review of agency budgets. Requests that are not thoroughly justified and programmed tend either to be discarded or fully formulated before the executive budget is submitted.

A second result is the fiscal education of the legislature or, at least, of a small part of it. A body aware of the implications of the budget will review it more carefully while giving attention to the programs of state government as well as itemized details of expenditure. Policy decisions tend thereby to be made consciously and not by default. For example, in Wisconsin, millions of dollars were saved as a result of legislative budget staff review. In one year seventy recommendations were made by the staff to the Joint Finance Committee. Twenty-nine of these were accepted in precisely the form proposed by the staff. Another fourteen were modified in some respect by the committee. Reliable estimates place the amount saved by the committee as a result of the staff recommendations at $9.5 mililon.

Third, the process of sharing information helps create better working relationships between the executive and legislative branches and will effect the communication and coordination necessary for the efficient execution of the state's business. State agencies have an avenue of appeal, since they will not be limited entirely to the necessary restrictions imposed on them by executive budget watchers. In a word, liaison will be established.

By strengthening the legislature's role in the budget-making process, a fiscal review agency also ultimately strengthens the executive's role in the same process. The two forces interacting produce a synthesis of informed views. Without this interaction, which the Founding Fathers called "checks and balances," Americans cannot claim to have coordinate government in the states.

PART THREE

A Crucial Factor to Legislative Reform: Personnel

Difficult though it may be, the issue of personnel in the state governments must be faced. State government woefully lacks the talent that is available on the national level. The drain of bright, young people can be partially attributed to the de-emphasis on state government by the teachers of American universities. For too long, talented students have been taught to believe the only opportunity for service is at the federal level. Furthermore, the states have not tried to lure talent by making salaries and conditions competitive. Also, conditions are such that those who do choose to serve in the legislature are placed in a difficult position. In this part, Chapter Eight shows the problems of the legislators themselves, while Chapter Nine describes the problems of acquiring and training professionals in government. Both chapters demonstrate the importance of the proper use of a free government's chief resource—namely, its people.

Legislative Ethics and Conflict of Interest

The American democratic form of government has from the start been committed to the principle of citizen participation in government. By this it is not meant that citizens are expected simply to participate in the discussion of public policy or to cast an intelligent vote. Rather, it means the system of citizen-lawmakers, citizen-governors, and citizen-judges.

For example, consider a man who more or less reflects his particular social environment. He is educated, ethical, financially independent, and as able as the segment of the populace from which he is drawn. He is elected to office or appointed to the court, and is expected to write laws and enforce them; in short, he is expected to govern.

The resulting product has been the subject of debate through the ages and culminates in a remark attributed to Winston Churchill: "Democracy is clearly the worst form of government ever invented except all the others which have been tried so far."

When the common man is elected or appointed to public office, he is immediately and inevitably thrown into a cross fire of conflicts of interest. His job can be described as one of balanc-

Source: Adapted from a speech given by Jess Unruh at the Eagleton Legislator's Seminar, Naples, Florida, July 24, 1969.

ing the interests of all the forces in society seeking representation. He is part and parcel of a certain number of those interests, and there must inescapably be a conflict between his private and public roles. Perhaps the only way for the public official to avoid the nagging fear that he may get caught up in such a conflict, and to avoid the constant public inference that the general interest has been sold out, is to do as the Kennedy family has done (to choose an example on the federal level). One generation devotes its talents and energies to amassing a fortune. The fortune is put in trust for the second generation so that generation can be totally free of the burden of making a living or increasing its wealth. That second generation is then able to apply itself to public service without a guilty conscience. We have been extremely fortunate in this country to have gotten, as a result of this process, so able, so courageous, and so effective a President as John F. Kennedy and such outstanding senators as Robert F. and Edward M. Kennedy.

Can we *always* be so sure that the sons of wealthy families will prove that capable? Have we reached the point that only the scions of the wealthy can participate in public affairs?

But the Kennedy and Rockefeller families are exceptions to the rule, which holds generally that the sons of extremely successful men are rarely as able as their fathers. A further irony is that *the very ability* that it takes to cultivate a fortune might otherwise be available for public affairs. Fortunately, Americans are not content to restrict government to an aristocracy of wealth. It is regarded as too narrow a group from which to draw public servants. Democracy does not lend itself to management by an elite.

The alternative is that the man who serves in office must also make a living. How can he do justice to both the public welfare and his own welfare without violating either?

All of the problems raised here are complicated and made worse by the low salaries paid to legislators, as was discussed in Chapter One. Generally, an individual who is elected to the legislature is of such a caliber that he is capable of earning much more than the amount he draws as a legislator and is entitled by his abilities to live on a standard higher than his public office provides. To earn an adequate income the legislator today in many states must still devote much, if not most, of his time to his private business. Therefore in most cases, he thinks of himself primarily as a lawyer, teacher, or insurance man, and only secondarily as a legislator. Some professionals are excluded entirely from legislative service until they have reached a relatively high level of economic success in their private pursuits. Although the larger states have somewhat moved away from this by paying better salaries and even relatively good pensions, they too have many problems.

Americans do recognize this problem in the judicial branch of government. By providing judges with an adequate scale of pay, we can afford them the opportunity for the independence and dignity that should avoid the necessity for conflict and is in keeping with the noble purpose of their profession.

Let us turn to some examples that confront the citizen-public servant, particularly the problem of the lawyer-legislator. He spends part of the year enacting laws. The remainder of his time is spent in trying to make a living practicing law. Then there is the problem of practicing before state commissions or boards, seeking information for his client from state agencies or departments. If the lawyer-legislator calls on a state official and asks him to reverse the rules, or just to bend them on behalf of his client, it is relatively easy to agree that he is engaged in a conflict of interest, at least, and possibly a great deal more. But, what if he calls the director of a state agency and simply asks for information on behalf of his client? He may have authored legislation that created the agency or amended its statutory authority. He may have influenced the governor in the selection of the incumbent director. If he is a committee chairman he may have legislation important to that department pending before his committee. Is he engaged in a conflict then?

Can any lawyer-legislator practice before any state court without running the risk of conflict? Did he vote to create the very court in which he appears? Did he recommend the appointment of the judge? Will he, in the future, vote on the salary increase of that judge?

Some of the problems raised by the call from the legislator to the department or agency on behalf of his constituent exist even when he is *not* a lawyer. *Occasionally* the state official will attempt to give the legislator a favorable reply in an effort to curry favor when the legislator has not asked for this advantage. In short, there is virtually nothing one can do as a member of the legislature that does *not* constitute a conflict of interest.

Some legislators attempt to meet this problem by a kind of scrupulous honesty which can best be described as "saintly." Some have made it a standing practice to return every gift, no matter how small, to the sender. Others, such as attorneys, have made an honest effort to avoid taking on any clients who came to them because of their governmental connection. Some of these people have left the legislature because they were unable to support their families on the combination of legislative pay and legal fees.

Today it is rare for a legislator's vote to be corrupted by the exchange of money. Far more often the integrity of the vote is shattered by a commitment to a particular interest group, resulting from a lack of independence on the part of the legislator for a variety of nonfinancial reasons. For example, a vote may be influenced for reasons of idealogy or fear of antagonizing the voting strength of a particular group. One who is overly committed to labor or to management, or to any other interest group, whatever his reasons, can be charged with being as guilty of selling out the public interest as the man who takes money for his vote. Yet how can one search a man's mind to determine what prompted his vote?

It is interesting how much "image" continues to play a part in politics. Perhaps it escalates in importance as more and more people view their politicians on television, but a small percentage see them personally. A nationally noted journalist, speaking during the general election campaign of 1960 about this, paraphrased Machiavelli about President Eisenhower. Eisenhower, he said, would leave office having accepted more gifts than any other president in American history—gifts which would total more than a million dollars. Yet he had such an aura of honesty and integrity that this had almost no impact on his general image with the American people.

Machiavelli's view was that it was more important for the Prince to *seem* honest than for him to *be* honest. This is a fact of political life that has figured strongly in forming the position taken by this author on disclosure laws, about which more will be said later. Today politicians still rely very much on image making, often of the negative kind, by trying to establish that the opposition is corrupt. This kind of "purity potlatch," as Dean Bayless Manning of Stanford's Law School describes it, is generally only feasible in the context of a particular election and its contestants. Some politicians simply cannot be portrayed as corrupt or injured by tales of corruption, no matter how often such tales are repeated. Their image is so well established that it cannot be materially affected by that kind of a campaign.

A recent well-publicized incident in California emphasizes

this point. It was revealed that a state senator, chairman of a powerful committee stood to benefit by some $200,000 because of an appreciation of stock in an insurance company which had only a short time before being defunct. Supposedly he had gotten permission from the insurance commissioner to revive the company by introducing legislation that would have severely cut the commissioner's staff. Although the commissioner denied that this action had anything to do with his subsequent decision this was the general assumption. Interestingly, the senator could not have benefitted had the decision not been made. But the commissioner and the head of the executive branch of government have received curiously little criticism, even though both have defended the decision and the governor defended his commissioner. This interesting situation devolves from two sources: (1) the general low image of the legislative branch and (2) the general feeling that the governor is a "good guy" who may make unintentional mistakes because he is not a political professional but is a sort of citizen-governor with no intent to personally profit therefrom.

For the first few years of a legislative career the problem and the opportunity for straying is not very consequential and so it is ranked far down on the list of priorities. Not much is expected of new, young legislators either by way of political results or subscription to the ways of success. It is usually after a legislator achieves a measure of success that the problem begins to assume major significance. It may arise earlier in smaller states where outside income constitutes a major part (or, in some cases, most) of a legislator's take-home pay. In those cases it seems the problem is much more difficult to deal with and it is not so easy to make hard and fast rules.

The life of a legislator is further complicated by a fact that, to our knowledge, exists only in politics:

> In every other profession that I am aware of, success is accompanied by relatively similar financial success. Not so in politics, and particularly the legislative branch of politics. The indolent legislator receives the same pay as the industrious, and the visible lawmaker from whom much is expected receives no more than the anonymous one from whom nothing is expected. Successful men are expected by this society to do certain things. They cannot wear rags or go to fourth-rate hotels. They are expected to entertain to some degree or other, even their wives must dress in a certain style. When these demands are not

accompanied by financial return from the legislative occupation, they must be met by funds from other sources.[1]

The preceding is the explanation for the myriad of "slush" funds that have been witnessed over the years from the 1952 Nixon fund to today when any rising politician who does not have huge personal financial resources is probably at a serious disadvantage. It stems from America's reluctance to face the real costs of government directly and a willingness to ignore these problems. This means that the costs are met indirectly, almost always semisecretly, and generally by a relatively few persons or interests. How does one live in this milieu and maintain any degree of independence while climbing the ladder of success?

Honest men cannot be legislated. It may be that Americans must accept honesty as a postulate in politics, as in other professions. There is much evidence that there is at least as much honesty and integrity in politics as in other professions; possibly there is more. The answer lies in two directions, one specific, one general.

There is an old saying that there are no secrets in politics. If some enterprising reporter or an aggressive opponent desires to investigate thoroughly enough, he can usually find out even the most well hidden information. The danger lies in the fact that if this is the way the information is derived, it will be presented as the total picture. This fact, plus others, have led this author to believe strongly in full disclosure of holdings, income, *and* campaign contributions. It is far better that *all* of the facts are laid bare than to rely upon one's opposition or the press to divulge part of them.

While full disclosure may not materially affect the probity of the legislative branch, it will seem to do so with the general public, which, as Machiavelli said, may be more important. This is particularly necessary now with the move to increase the capacity of the legislative branch. As cases of individual cupidity are exposed in the legislature (and this will probably continue at some level at least) there is little defense for the legislature as an institution. If full disclosure were operative this would provide some line of institutional defense. Disclosure should of course apply to challengers for office as well as in-

---

[1] From a talk given by Jess Unruh at the University of Texas, November 1963.

cumbents. The two or three states that have required full disclosure have not yet proven anything very permanently except that the system still works despite some discomfort to a few individuals. A statute forbidding a legislator (or judge or executive) from engaging in activities that constitute a major conflict is also desirable.

Beyond these measures, there are a few other things to add in the way of general approaches. Proper decision-making tools are perhaps more valuable in avoiding conflicts than is almost any legislation. William Pincus of the Ford Foundation states accurately that most corruption occurs because only a very few are privy to the situation wherein it occurs. Add a few bright young staff people to a committee, he says, and the chances of keeping the secret are greatly diminished while the chances of apprehension of the wrongdoers are enhanced.

Ambition and visibility are also major deterrents to the kind of old-fashioned vote buying that Jay Gould boasted of in the late nineteenth century. The politician who is looking for support for his next step is far less likely to be involved in personal financial dishonesty than his stagnating colleague.

There is no single answer for everyone in every situation. The final answer will again usually be a variation of Machiavelli's theme. Is the officeholder credible to the public? The other, less obvious answer is whether he can live with himself.

Writing on a personal level, I have, in my career, served as Speaker, chairman of the Appropriations Committee, chairman of the Finance and Insurance Committee, and now as Minority Leader. I have also managed two gubernatorial campaigns, a presidential campaign, several presidential primaries, acted as chief fund-raiser for legislative Democrats and gotten myself reelected seven times. I doubt that I have hewed to a constant line in just my own thinking much less my actions.

I have not become so antiseptic that I have not made money on outside ventures or activities. Conversely I have tried to confine moneymaking to activities which *may* have occurred *because* of my office but not by *use* of my office—a subtle distinction perhaps but an important one. In a part-time legislature particularly, I do not think we can expect our legislators to forswear every opportunity for personal gain. What we should expect is that they not *use* their office for that.

This is not suggested as the perfect answer, but until we are willing to pay directly the costs of government; until our salaries, pensions, and working conditions are far beyond what they are now and until the people are willing to properly and directly finance campaigns it is suggested as the best we can do. Success will be largely like the success of our monetary system— only as good as the people believe it is.

CHAPTER NINE

State Legislative Interns

Disillusionment too often comes to college students who are "lucky" enough to be chosen as state legislative interns. They have been picked from among their peers because they have shown special promise in their academic and campus political life and they look forward to the chance to see politics in action from close up. They arrive at the state house full of hope and enthusiasm at the beginning of the summer. When many of them leave at the end of August, they feel bitterly cheated.

In between, they have experienced little of the vital political activity they had come to see. Instead they find themselves assigned to dingy basement rooms running mimeograph machines or typing stacks of staff-prepared routine answers to letters from constituents. If they have met the legislator to whom they were assigned, it may have been only a brief introduction on the first day. Missing from their exposure to practical politics is an understanding of internal legislative politics, of the variety of demands made by a legislator upon his personal staff, of the importance and power structure of the committee staff in the legislature,

Source: Adapted from a paper prepared by Donald G. Herzberg for a conference on interns, Puerto Rico, April 1961, sponsored by the American Political Science Association.

or of a legislative or investigative committee in executive session.

Internships probably fail more due to inadvertence than to a lack of understanding of the purposes of intern programs. Perhaps the whole situation could be avoided if legislators and their staffs would keep the objectives of internships in mind. Basically, there are two objectives. The first is to provide the student with a firsthand knowledge of government operations, or at least a small area of governmental responsibility, so that he might be a better student, potential teacher of the political process, or perhaps even a future participant in government service. The second objective is to demonstrate to the administrative, legal, and political units of government that not only is there an immediate value in intern contributions to the work of the agency, but that ultimately it would be desirable to put more emphasis on the professionalization of staff members. The effectiveness of these programs depends upon their administration.

The administration of an internship program involves a variety of problems because of the nature of the program's objective—bringing together the worlds of the student and the practitioner. In order to bring about the most successful union of these two worlds, it is absolutely vital to have a university or college sympathetic to the goals of the intern program, as well as good students, a knowledgeable faculty advisory, and, of course, a state governmental unit not only willing to take an intern but also aware of the limitations of the program. Rare, indeed, is the intern program that has all of these factors and is operating near an optimum level. The critical factors covered in this chapter are: the problems of the colleges and universities as they struggle to create intern programs; the problems of the faculty coordinator who must run the program; the problems of the intern himself; and the problems of the government legislative offices to which interns receive appointments.

Unlike medical internships or law clerkships, which are an integral part of the formal educational process, colleges and universities tend to discount internships in the social sciences. They are not part of the general trend of formal academic studies and there is considerable sentiment that they should not be.

Exceptions to this doubtlessly exist, and they have usually been found in undergraduate courses in which participant observation is part of the required work. Because the undergraduate carries a full academic course of regular class hours, little time remains in which he may fully participate. At best he may become involved in a local campaign in the fall or visit the mayor's office weekly. American universities and colleges simply are not geared toward allowing students to participate for long periods of time during the regular semesters. Even institutions with summer intern programs have made little effort to work out academic credit for the student's experience. Undergraduate intern programs, in general, have not convinced social science faculties and college administrators that they merit academic credits. Many faculty members, while reasonably convinced of the general value of these programs, nevertheless feel that they should be regarded as enrichment opportunities rather than as worthy of academic credit.

With regard to graduate intern programs, the hostility of universities toward the granting of academic credit for intern programs becomes even more apparent. Here the failure to appreciate the goals of an intern program are more serious and certainly more damaging. Because graduate internships are usually of a longer duration than undergraduate ones, it is difficult to convince graduate students that it is worthwhile to give the time an internship demands. Beset with time limits for pursuit of graduate degrees, many students are unwilling to lose more time. This is especially so if students are led to believe that the university, by its failure to give credit, is lukewarm to the idea of an internship.

Many of the universities and organizations responsible for the development of intern programs have attempted to set up academic seminars in connection with the intern's job assignment. In spite of the high caliber of these seminars, the participants have been unable for the most part to earn formal academic credit for their work.

In some cases several universities band together in an intern program; an attempt is made to avoid the issue of academic credit entirely. The following announcement of a legislative intern program is typical: "This program does not, in itself, provide any academic credit. It may be possible, however, for these assistantships to be considered as recognized field study or internship for candidates whose course of study requires such an assignment. The final decision on the acceptability of an assistantship for credit will rest with the students' university." Or sometimes the problem is stated this way: "The intern will be registered at one of the recognized colleges or universities giving graduate degrees. The decision to give academic credit will be determined by each institution."

Further difficulties arise in the administration of programs that involve two universities. In order to assure continuity and reasonable administration, one university must assume final responsibility for the program. That university selects one man to run the program and he will have to take special pains not to act arbitrarily. He will have to keep the interested faculty of the other school closely informed of his activity and work with them in the development of policy. The faculty member in charge must be especially careful not to favor his university or his students in the program. A special problem arises in the management of summer undergraduate programs. Here, relations between the cooperating institutions must be particularly smooth so that no institution appears to be gaining an advantage either in numbers of interns placed or the type of positions arranged.

In the case of multi-institution involvement in intern programs, the groups usually select a multiuniversity committee with a single faculty chairman to govern the program. The selection is determined by the focus of power, and that usually rests with the group controlling the financial resources. If an outside foundation or organization has made a grant, they will hold the power. On the other hand, if no outside grant has been made or if it has been made for the use of several institutions it will be necessary to work out ground rules for multi-institution participation. When financing is not localized at one particular institution, a rotating chairmanship seems advisable.

The greatest difficulty facing these academic committees is the development of appropriate guidelines for the selection of interns. There is a tendency to rely on criteria developed for the awarding of more conventional fellowships and assistant-ships. These criteria are not always relevant to the selection of individuals for internships in political or governmental agencies. Using similar academic criteria as a starting point, additional emphasis should be placed on special skills, talents, and qualities required of a political intern. It is these requirements—a greater degree of extrovertism, an enhanced ability to write clearly, succinctly, and under pressure, a commitment to politics, and an appreciation of the role of the politician—that are rarely reflected in the present criteria governing selection of academic fellows.

The selection committees are not always composed entirely of academicians but sometimes have a few nonacademic members representing the administrative and political units that the interns will be entering. The government and political members can be useful in stressing and recognizing the special qualities that are necessary in a political intern. They are likely, however, to be handicapped in that the academic standards that must be imposed may not be very meaningful to them.

It is useful, of course, to have the academic officer who will be responsible for the administration of the program sit on the committee. This gives him an opportunity early in the process to be alerted to possible problems as he negotiates with both the nonacademic members and with colleagues from other institutions.

Following is the way that the sponsoring committee of the Illinois intern program was officially set up some years ago:

> There is hereby created a sponsoring committee for Legislative staff internships, which shall consist of the chairman of the Legislative Council *ex officio*. 2 Senators appointed by the President Pro tempore of the Senate, 2 Representatives appointed by the Speaker of the House, and 5 academic members named from cooperating universities, respectively, by the presidents of Northwestern University, Illinois Institute of Technology, the University of Illinois, and Southern Illinois University, and the chancellor of the University of Chicago. Members shall serve until July 1 of each odd-numbered year and until their successors are appointed and qualified, except that General Assembly members shall serve such term or until termination of their legislative service, whichever first occurs. Succors shall be appointed during the month of June in each odd-numbered year. Vacancies shall be filled by appointment for the unexpired term in the same manner as original appointments. Appointments shall be in writing and filed with the Secretary of State as a public record. A program coordinator for legislative staff internships shall serve as Secretary of the sponsoring committee without vote.

> *Rule 1.*   The Committee shall hold four regular meetings during each biennium as follows: (a) in Chicago on the last Tuesday of October of odd-numbered years, (b) in Springfield on the last Tuesday of March of every year, and (c) in Springfield on the third Tuesday of November in even-numbered years, provided it may hold special meetings at other times and places in lieu of regular meetings. Special meetings may be called by the

Committee or by the Chairman, specifying the time and place. The Secretary shall notify members at least five days in advance of each meeting.

Rule 2. At its meeting in each October of odd-numbered years, the Committee shall elect a Chairman and Vice Chairman from among its members. The Chairman shall be from the legislative membership of the Committee; the Vice Chairman shall be from the academic membership. The program coordinator shall serve as secretary without a vote.

Rule 3. The Committee shall adopt a statement of policy to be followed by the program coordinator in the administration of the legislative staff internship program and for the guidance of legislative agencies and commissions desiring to utilize the the services of legislative interns.

Rule 4. In addition to any reports required by the statement of policy, the program coordinator shall submit to the Committee at its November meeting in even-numbered years, a draft of a report to be submitted to the General Assembly. Copies of this report, after any changes by the Committee and when approved by it, shall be submitted to the membership of the General Assembly.[1]

Another problem that often confronts the selection committee is dealing with the diverse backgrounds of intern applicants. Undergraduates with majors in a variety of fields, such as English, economics, history, political science, sociology, and psychology, may make the selection for a limited number of positions difficult. One requirement is absolutely necessary: the ability to write well.

The problem of diverse backgrounds and preparations becomes more involved on the graduate level because of the differences in preparation among graduate students, law students, and students of journalism. This diversity of background may cause difficulties not only in the original selection of candidates but also in the choice of seminar content once the program has commenced.

It cannot be emphasized too strongly how critical the right choice of a faculty adviser is to the success of an intern program. A good adviser is one who has the respect of his colleagues even though they may have reservations about intern programs. He must have the respect of the personnel of the agencies with which he deals. Ideally, he should be both a scholar and a man who may have had some experience as a governmental or po-

---

[1] Illinois Revised Statutes, 1963, Chap. 63, Sect. 42.1–42.4.

litical adviser himself. Above all else, he must have a high degree of sensitivity both to his students and to the people for whom they work. He should not view legislators as "pieces of data."

The faculty adviser has a series of responsibilities. Usually, he is the person who makes the arrangements for the specific work assignments of the interns. At the undergraduate level, this means working with a variety of people in a variety of agencies. At the graduate level, it may simply involve working with one staff person or one politician who then makes the specific assignments. In either case, the faculty adviser must keep himself informed of what the positions are and know enough about the specific job situation to be helpful to his students as they come to the jobs.

The adviser must also keep his academic colleagues and the members of the selection committee informed. This takes special effort in the multiuniversity program and can be the difference between success and failure. The adviser needs to communicate the students' progress, their triumphs, and their failures.

A sensitive adviser must be able to define the situation in which his intervention is ultimately necessary. The general rule should be to intervene as little as possible in the job situations of the intern. On rare occasions, however, because of a mismatch of intern with job, a clash of personalities, or a complete misunderstanding of the role of an intern, problems do arise that require tactful but fast action. On occasion, a discussion between the adviser and the agency personnel rather than direct intervention, will correct a problem or misunderstanding. The adviser is the buffer and he must often be available to both the student and the agency.

One of the greatest difficulties of intern programs stems directly from failure of the faculty adviser to discuss adequately with his agency counterpart the academic goals of an intern program. It is even more useful if the faculty adviser has the opportunity to discuss these goals with everyone who will be directly involved with the intern. For instance, one graduate legislative intern program ran into difficulties because the interns were seen sitting in the legislative gallery listening to the proceedings rather than working. For this they were severely criticized by legislative personnel unfamiliar with the intern program. Fortunately, the alert faculty adviser heard about the criticism and quickly took steps to explain that this kind of observation was an essential part of the interns' program. He further displayed his sensitivity and political acumen by suggesting to the interns that in the future they should not sit in the gallery en masse and should refrain from applauding the speeches of legislators whom they favored.

A final responsibility of the faculty adviser is applicable only in those intern programs that include a regularly scheduled academic seminar, sometimes for credit, with the interns. Given the diversity of the job experiences the interns are likely to have, it takes a great deal of ingenuity to arrange a seminar that will be helpful and meaningful to the interns. If the seminar is for academic credit, how much time would the interns have to devote to reading and research? Whether for credit or not, how far would the faculty member go in making the seminar more vocationally oriented? For instance, if one is operating a seminar for legislative interns, should the seminar be arranged around the operation of that one state legislature or should it broadly encompass the legislative process? Should the thrust of the seminar rest on the bringing in of a stream of outside speakers, such as legislators, staff people, budget officers, and other representatives of the executive branch?

Seminars that are academic in nature and broad in their approach are often met with derogatory comments on the part of the intern, at least at the time of his internship. Many interns, however, forget that they are still part of an academic enterprise. They also tend to become so involved in the daily tasks at hand and so wrapped up in the "headlines" of their job situation that they may lose their perspective. They minimize the value of their academic experience and become convinced that what they learn from their job experience is more important than it really is. In some cases, when interns are placed in scattered positions around the state, a prefield seminar is useful. At this seminar, some briefing may be given as to what to expect and the role of the participant observer is analyzed. A postfield seminar in which the interns discuss their experience is also helpful.

We have witnessed the mushrooming of state intern programs throughout the country at both the undergraduate as well as the graduate level. The great number of these programs underscores one of the inherent weaknesses of any internship: the failure of the intern to bring to his position sufficient background to perform his job satisfactorily. While there are many exceptions, the fact remains that many colleges and universities simply do not give students adequate coursework in American politics or state and local government. These inadequacies quickly become apparent when the student is put in an intern position. Not only must the intern have an adequate academic background, but it is vitally important that he be given a thorough briefing about the particular position he will take. Only in this way, when there is complete understanding of the situation, can the intern be expected to operate successfully.

The working relationship developed between intern and supervisor is critical. Only in the most fortunate of circumstances does an intern arrive at an office and achieve instant rapport with his supervisor and the other members of the governmental family with whom he will be dealing. It is essential to the relationship, however, that the intern gain the confidence of his supervisor. The auspices under which he comes into the office may be useful. Obviously, however, there is no real way to teach a person how to gain the influence of another. Common sense and judgment must prevail, as well as a willingness to work hard for long hours.

Occasionally, special problems arise that make establishing rapport and gaining acceptance more difficult. In placing students in political offices, a basic rule for intern programs should be that the intern be of the same political persuasion as the officer for whom he is to work. This rule should be followed in legislative internships as well. This cannot always be the case; there have been wholesale violations of the rule. Situations have arisen in which all of the interns chosen were of the party opposing that of their supervisor. In one such situation, the political maturity, sophistication, and sense of humor of the legislative officer allowed him to work with the interns and persuade them of his inherent worth. The question was raised as to how the interns were able to work with a majority leader who was basically a deep conservative. The students informed the questioner that he failed to understand how great the politician really was. In other situations, however, intern programs have suffered when the student and the practitioner have no common ground.

Another complication arises, again particularly in legislative or political programs, when some of the interns are from out of state. Out-of-state interns need extra preparation in order to prove that they can be useful on the job as in-state interns. The National Center for Education in Politics' graduate intern program has had extraordinary success in placing out-of-state students in governors' and mayors' offices. Success here can only be achieved by placing carefully selected interns in offices where there is an awareness of the purposes of the program and a willingness to educate the intern. It may be useful when interns are going to out-of-state positions to have them subscribe to local newspapers prior to their arrival. As a general rule, however, intern programs do not lend themselves easily to out-of-state personnel. This is particularly true of legislative internships, in which the problems of adjustment are serious enough without the added disability of nonresidence.

The length of time that an intern is to serve is another factor that affects the program. Undergraduate summer internships tend to be about eight weeks in duration. This is a sufficient length of time for the undergraduate to gain a basic knowledge of an office, but it is not really long enough for the intern to make any substantial contribution to the functioning of the office. Since the latter is not one of the major functions of an undergraduate program, this is not serious.

Graduate internships, however, usually run one semester and sometimes two. A semester is barely long enough to provide the intern with a meaningful experience or give the office another experienced employee. Certainly, no graduate program should ever be less than one semester.

Another aspect of the time factor in internship programs is the question of when they should operate. Summer is a traditional time for undergraduate programs. However, in many ways it is the worst time to place a student because the pace of many offices slows down considerably and key personnel may be off on vacations.

The timing of graduate intern programs is somewhat more appropriate. Most of these programs begin in September and run to the end of January. Occasionally, they start with the winter semester and run through June. The yearlong legislative internships normally commence in September. These interns have an opportunity to move slowly into the legislative mill and to prepare themselves for the January onslaught.

A critical problem in connection with legislative interns involves those who serve in states in which the legislature normally meets every second year. Clearly, the experience and the value of the experience is different for an intern who serves his term in a session year from that of an intern who works in the nonsession year. Normally, interns in off years are assigned to the legislative council or to a legislative committee to work on special problems of research. Except in unusual cases, the experience gained differs little from executive branch experience, except that the pace of the legislative enterprise may be a bit slower.

With regard to placement, interns themselves agree that they prefer to have a specific assignment in an office rather than to be involved in a pool operation. A pool arrangement, in which interns have the opportunity for a wide variety of experiences working for a number of different men, does give broader knowledge. However, psychological and prestige factors become involved and interns find it more satisfactory to establish themselves with just one man. There is agreement, however, that the wider the variety of assignments given to the intern within the framework of a single office, the better.

A common problem is that of achieving the proper job level. In many instances faulty advance work has compelled the male intern to start off as a glorified office boy and the female intern to start as a stenographer and file clerk. Convincing the office staff that the intern has a different role to play is difficult to do. Office personnel are sometimes suspicious of academic "types" and many enjoy "taking them down a peg." Generally, good nature and a willingness to pitch in when an office crisis looms can help convince the office personnel that the intern is in a professional or semiprofessional role. The intern's supervisor can alleviate the problem by providing sufficient work to keep the intern busy. Then he simply does not have time to stuff envelopes or fetch the coffee.

There are times, particularly at the beginning of an internship, when students may not have enough work to keep them busy. All offices have such periods and not all supervisors are good at creating work assignments. In the beginning, there may be some justifiable doubts as to the actual abilities of the intern to do certain jobs. If the intern is involved in a political internship (if not in a political assignment, he is usually with a political person) it may be useful for the intern to produce some analysis of electoral data. All politicians are fascinated by research of this kind and many are totally unfamiliar with the magic that can be worked by weaving election results with census tract data. In administrative internships, there are always scores of annual reports that can be read to give the intern insight and background into his assignment. If the intern still hasn't enough work after two or three weeks, the academic supervisor ought to be consulted.

Interns often find great difficulty in keeping an interest in and in providing the time for their work for the academic seminar. As the *Fourth Annual Report of the California Legislative Program* stated, "For some interns, the seminar continued to be a strain; the workload of some was sufficiently heavy at times to interfere with their ability to participate fully in seminar sessions and preparation. Some experienced a reduction in motivation to engage in serious academic work. After several years as students, they were happy to have a job and preferred to be free of academic obligations." Despite the dissatisfactions with the seminars while on the job, former interns who presently are in academic positions strongly defend the seminar. Many of them would argue for an even more academically oriented seminar. The feeling is less strong among former interns who stayed in government service, or became lawyers or journalists. Even among this group, however, there is a general mellowing and concession that the seminar did serve to tie things together.

A special problem is faced by interns who are using their intern experience to do research and gather data for academic purposes. It is the problem of maintaining confidentiality in regard to the information gathered while in a privileged position. The problem is sharpened when privileged information is a vital part of a student's research. A sensible rule would be that if the information gained could not have been gained in any other way, or if his supervisor feels that the information revealed would be damaging or embarrassing, the student may not include it. If, however, he is able to work out satisfactory ground rules for the inclusion of the material, fine. If he cannot work out such rules, he is committed not to include it.

By way of summarizing the problems of the intern, there is the paramount matter of role conflicts. Again, the *4th Annual Report* is useful:

> Role conflicts and uncertainties continue to be of considerable importance. Neither interns, nor legislators, nor legislative staff are entirely certain where interns fit into the scheme of things. For the intern, some psychological strain arises from the fact that a number of agencies have a part in the administration of the Internship Program—the Rules Committee, the Speaker's Office, the chairman or other officer to whom he is assigned and members of his staff, the Executive Committee, and the faculty supervisor. The intern has to be responsive to the differing, although usually not incompatible expectations of all of these individuals and agencies. The most important role strain arises from differing emphases as to the intern's status: Is he primarily a student or is he primarily a full-time legislative assistant?

Nearly everyone concerned recognizes both roles, but their relative importance and significance is viewed in different ways in different quarters—and even the interns themselves do not see "eye to eye."

Obviously this is a vital problem that calls for understanding and tact on the part of all involved.

Certainly many of the problems posed in the discussion of adviser and intern could be recast as the same problems faced by the supervisor on the job. He is equally concerned with demands of the academic seminars, particularly, as always seems to be the case, when an office crisis coincides with the meeting time of the seminar. The supervisor, when he does hand out an assignment, is concerned with the proper completion of the work. He feels great concern about the uses an intern may put to the confidential information he has learned on the job. The supervisor, more than anyone else, has the responsibility for seeing that the intern works at the proper level.

One of the most common roles the supervisor must play is that of the broker or the mediator. To be successful, he must fully understand the nature of the intern's position and interpret it to members of his staff and to members of a larger public, either at large or within the agency. Unfortunately, the supervisor faces a shortage of time. Time is what he must give to the intern if the intern is to be properly oriented. The supervisor, ideally, should be prepared to sacrifice more of his own time, for hopefully he too believes in the vitality of young new interns who one day may be where he is now. Truly, the outcome of any intern program is affected by the use the politician's staff makes of the intern.

If the experience is a good one the politician will come to recognize the kind of contribution that professionals can make directly to operation, and the intern, either as a teacher with his students or as a student communicating to other students, will bring back a picture of politics and government as a stimulating and honorable way of life. Both, hopefully, will increase the movement of well-trained and highly dedicated people into public service. Should this be the result—even in small measure —of the various intern programs, they will have more than justified the time, money, and work involved.

PART FOUR

What Has Been Done?

The first three parts of this volume have discussed the process, problems, and prescriptions relevant to American state legislatures. The territory we have covered is in no way virgin land. States have been grappling with all of this in various ways throughout the years, with real impetus coming only recently. Our purpose in Chapter Ten is to describe some of the history of this movement and to present a number of workable reforms. It is encouraging to see the number of viable advancements actually being made, as well as those attempted, in the area of the state legislative process. We hope that this trend continues and that in the near future state governments will become more attuned to deal with the problems of today and to prevent the problems of tomorrow.

CHAPTER TEN

Legislative Reform: An Overview

The cause of state legislative improvement has become increasingly popular over the last few years. Some call it modernization; some call it reform; some call it upgrading. Whatever it is called, it amounts to the same thing: a desire to propel state legislatures into the twentieth century. One of the more familiar formulations of the problem has been how to transform the horse-and-buggy legislatures into modern, competent, supersonic, decision-making vehicles.

The origins of this movement are difficult to pinpoint exactly. Individual state legislators and occasional scholars have been writing about the problem periodically since the mid-1930s. It is now generally conceded that the main impetus dates from about the time of the Supreme Court decisions in the reapportionment cases. This is not to say that the Supreme Court decisions were the *cause* of legislative reform. Changes were beginning to take place in the direction of modernizing the legislative system before those decisions were rendered. But the same forces and pressures that brought about the Supreme Court decisions (the rapid transformation of American society from

Source: Prepared by Jess Unruh and Donald G. Herzberg especially for this volume.

rural to urban) were operating on the state legislatures to begin the process of making them responsive to the problems generated by a rapidly growing, complex, urban and urbane society.

Although we may not know exactly how this movement got started, we do know that it has resulted in a mass of newspaper and magazine articles, a welter of speeches, and numerous reports and studies, most of which have been neglected. To realize the extent of possible reforms and methods available, one need only read one of these studies.

As far back as 1954, the American Political Science Association had Belle Zeller's definitive study *American State Legislatures* published.[1] Most of the recommendations are still valid. In 1961, the National Legislative Conference, an investigating body supported by the Council of State Governments, issued the final report and recommendations of its Committee on Legislative Processes and Procedures, *American State Legislatures in Mid-Twentieth Century*.[2] Every state has copies of that report; in a few states a portion of the recommendations have been implemented. But once again it remains a blueprint for modernization that has not yet been enacted. In that same year a printed discussion outline called *Improving Legislative Procedures*, used at the annual meeting of the National Conference of State Legislative Leaders, publicized many areas of legislative improvement that are still in the hopeful stage.

In 1963 the Committee on Organization of Legislative Service of the National Legislative Conference distributed its final report, *Mr. President . . . Mr. Speaker*. This, too, is available to all the states, and in 1966 the National Legislative Conference, by formal resolution, advised the states to utilize the information contained in it and other publications. Then, in 1967, came the report of the Committee for Economic Development; this report has perhaps, because of the prestige of the committee, received more widespread publicity than any of the others. Yet the recommendations are anything but new.

These publications were all widely distributed and most of them are still available. Furthermore, at least thirty states in recent years have undertaken studies of one kind or another concerned with staffing and organization, and have made spe-

---

[1] Belle Zeller, *American State Legislatures* (New York: Thomas Y. Crowell, 1954).

[2] *American State Legislatures in Mid-Twentieth Century* (Chicago, Ill.: Council of State Governments, April 1961).

cific recommendations. The first of a series was conducted for the state of New Jersey by the Eagleton Institute of Politics, which has also completed similar studies in six other states.

Thus no one can say that the movement for modernization of the legislature suffers from lack of information. The *what,* the *what's wrong,* and the *what ought to be done,* have been adequately covered, to say the least. Briefly, the goals set forth in all these studies and publications can be summarized under ten headings:

1. Legislative-executive relations need improvement in such areas as presession evolution of public policy and the preparation of the legislative program; appropriation of public funds and the postaudit of public expenditures; and review of administrative rules and decisions, retaining in the legislature some control over the powers that it delegates to administrative agencies.

2. Legislative sessions should be free of undue restriction in length of session, frequency of meetings, and subject matter to be discussed. In the 1970s, the proposition that all of a state's problems can be solved in a three-month session once every two years just does not seem workable, and indications are that the earlier proposed "solution" of holding one general session and one budget session in each biennium has not come up to the expectations of its proponents.

3. Legislative compensation should be specified by statute rather than by constitution, should probably reflect the responsibilities vested in a legislator (for example, as compared to the head of a division on the executive branch), and should be high enough to attract to legislative service qualified persons from all walks of life. In its study, the Committee for Economic Development stated that even in the smaller states the legislator's salary should be $15,000, while in larger states it might be set as high as $25,000.

4. Legislative staff should be selected on the basis of merit and competence. The type of information needed by a state legislature may differ from the information needs of the other two branches of state government, but the information needs of the policy-setting branch of state government are at least as critical as those of the administrative branch. The legislature should provide itself with sufficient (and full-time) staff so that it can meet its information needs on a continuing basis.

5. Legislative standing committees should be assigned broad functional areas of subject matter responsibility. This will make

it possible for their members to specialize and to develop expertise in the area of committee responsibility. To some degree (if the number of standing committees is held small enough) it will eliminate time conflicts in the committee schedule. The citizen interested in legislation will be better able to attend the hearings of importance to him. All major proposals should receive public hearings, and notices of public hearings should be published sufficiently early to enable interested parties to attend.

6. All legislative measures and amendments thereto should be printed. They should be available for distribution before public hearings are held. All legislative measures should, prior to printing, be inspected by a professional bill drafting staff. Where one legislature holds several successive sessions throughout its term of office, provision should be made for the carry-over of proposals from one session to the next throughout the term; this saves staff time, and printing time and costs. Every legislature should make adequate provision for the printing and distribution of new laws before they become effective.

7. State legislatures should explore all modern business machines and techniques for possible application to the legislative process. There are possibilities of improving the flow of legislative work by the adoption of machines to roll-call voting, reproduction of legislative measures, preparation of journals, indexing, bill status, information retrieval, statute law research, and recording of public hearings and legislative debates. With the text of the statutes stored in memory, computers can speed up bill typing, engrossing, enrolling, the publication of slip laws, and the editing and publication of the revised statutes.

8. Legislative finances—the funding of the operation of the legislature itself—are in need of review. State legislatures should provide themselves with appropriations adequate to meet all probable expenditures during a fiscal period. They should have exclusive control with responsibility.

9. Office facilities outside the chambers of the legislature, and sufficient staff individually assigned, should be available to every legislator. The measure of what is sufficient may differ with each state, but the members of state legislatures should not, as legislators, have to put up with working conditions that they would not tolerate in their private businesses or professions.

10. Orientation aids and presession seminars should offer to all members of state legislatures the opportunity to familiarize themselves—before the beginning of a new legislative term—

with the services available to them and the rules under which they will have to work.

This summary could, of course, be extended and probably is being extended in some of the states today. However, it covers the basic points that have been made.

One of the principal obstacles to achieving many of these fairly clear-cut goals is that in most states constitutional amendments are required. Recent election results provide cause for guarded optimism in assessing the public's willingness to accept legislative improvement.

Twelve states had constitutional amendments on the 1968 general election ballot that directly affected their legislatures. Virtually all of those proposals were for legislative improvement, ranging in scope from the carry-over of unfinished business from the even-year session to the odd-year session in New Jersey, to revision of the entire constitution in Florida. The major changes approved by the voters included the following:

Arizona: An increase in legislative salaries from $1800 to $6000 per year, and setting of the rate of legislative expense allowance by statute.

Florida: A new constitution that provides for annual legislative sessions and allows setting of legislative pay by statute.

Idaho: The establishment of annual sessions of the legislature.

Iowa: Annual sessions of the legislature, compensation and expense allowances to be set by statute, and an apportionment amendment that reduces the size of the Iowa Senate and House of Representatives to a maximum of fifty to one hundred members respectively.

Nebraska: An increase in legislative pay from $200 to $400 per month.

New Jersey: An amendment to allow unfinished business of the New Jersey legislature's even-year session to carry over to the odd-year session.

North Carolina: The power to set legislative compensation by statute.

Utah: The addition of an even-year budget session of twenty days to the current sixty-day biennial session, and an increase in legislative compensation from $250 per year and an expense allowance of $5 per day to a $25 per diem salary and $15 per diem expenses.

The preceding were the advances. The following were rejected by the voter.

Georgia: An amendment to increase the length of terms for members of the Georgia Senate and House of Representatives from two to four years.

Idaho: A proposal to remove specific legislative mileage allowance and compensation provisions from the constitution.

Montana: Lengthening the biennial session of the legislature from sixty to eighty days.

New Hampshire: Setting of legislative compensation by statute.

Texas: An increase of legislative pay from $4800 to $8400 per year.

In 1969, amendments in six states were considered, with little success. Those approved are the following.

Delaware: Six-month sessions of the legislature each year with no limitations as to subject matter.

Maine: The State senate be composed of an odd number of members in a chamber with between thirty-one and thirty-five senators.

Those defeated follow.

New Mexico: The legislature to set its own compensation, with no limitation on length of sessions, the ability to formulate its own rules, and the requirement that all legislative business be conducted in public.

Kentucky: The provision for annual sessions.

Texas: The establishment of a sixty-day session for fiscal matters in even-numbered years, and an increase in legislator's salaries from $4800 to $9800.

Maryland: The ability to extend sessions, and call special sessions, and the creation of a commission to set legislator's compensation.

The year 1970 holds much promise for nine American state legislatures where voters will consider these amendments:

Connecticut: Amendments to allow for annual sessions and special sessions.

Indiana: The provision by law for the length and frequency of sessions.

Nebraska: Provision for annual limited sessions.

Nevada: The adoption of annual sessions unrestricted

as to length or topic and the removal of the sixty-day limitation on compensation for legislators.

New Hampshire: The creation of a special commission to set the rate of legislative compensation.

Missouri: The addition of four-month even-year sessions to the current provision for a five-month session in odd-numbered years and the ability to set its own expense allowance, mileage, and number of secretaries.

North Carolina: An amendment that will allow the general assembly to call itself into special session.

Oregon: Allows for even-year sessions and the ability to call itself into special session.

West Virginia: The adoption of annual, general sixty-day sessions and an increase in salary from $1500 to $3000.

In addition, further constitutional revision that will affect state legislatures is going on in Indiana, Nebraska, Montana, South Dakota, Virginia, and Maryland.

Of course, constitutional amendment is only one of a number of ways to bring about legislative improvement. In a great many states, legislators themselves have taken the task in hand and by changing their rules, have made major strides forward in improving the operations of their respective houses. In Texas, under the leadership of Speaker Ben Barnes, dramatic changes were made entirely by means of alterations in the rules. The staffing that is being done in the Indiana Legislature is another example of changes brought about by the initiative of the legislative leadership.

Providing members with adequate space and supporting services, hiring competent staff, streamlining the committee system by creating fewer of them and dividing the workload reasonably and equitably among them—these and many other basic changes need to be made in order to modernize and improve the working of the legislature. In all but a very few states they can be made by action in the legislature alone, if there is the courage of leadership for doing it and the enlightenment among members to support and demand such leadership. There are now a number of national programs designed to assist state legislatures in the task of self-improvement and modernization. The great foundations, particularly Ford and Carnegie, have been extremely generous in their support of these efforts. The work being done by the National Municipal League, the Citizen's Commission for Improved Legislatures, the Eagleton Institute of Politics at Rutgers University, and the National Conferences of State Legislative Leaders, represents a most promising development in the long struggle for effective and responsive government.

When one contemplates this vast array of talent, resources, and institutional strength, it is difficult to believe these efforts will not succeed. Before we decide that victory is in sight, however, there are problems ahead and they should be faced squarely. There seems to be a disconcerting tendency on the part of all these legislative upgrading agencies to concentrate on the same phase of the problem despite the fact that all of these organizations or institutions have particular and distinctive capabilities. Each is in a position to contribute greatly to different segments of a complex and multifaceted set of concerns. Everyone seems to want to concentrate on the research and program development side of this enterprise and there appears to be developing a potential for jurisdictional disputes and claim jumping. Unless some reasonable efforts are made to create a rational division of labors and to direct traffic in an orderly manner, a great opportunity will deteriorate in duplication of effort and resulting confusion.

Certain organizations are best able to generate a desire for improvement on the part of legislators themselves (for example, the Legislative Leaders Conference). Others furnish the capacity to survey and plan (for example, the academic institutions). The groups that involve leaders of the business community are in the best position to generate public support, without which none of these efforts can hope to succeed. Unless some orderly method of coordination is developed, it is certain Americans will see their efforts thwarted by a curtailment of support of the foundations and other financial contributors, and a growing resistance from the legislatures themselves.

The great task of political leadership today is to convert the mass of raw knowledge that science and technology have produced into political settlements. The traditional political question, "What can we do?" is no longer apropos. The relevant question for political leaders to ask themselves is, "What do we *want* to do?" Almost anything is possible. There is hardly a problem known or imaginable for which we cannot foresee solutions in the reasonably near future. The tremendous danger is that these scientific achievements will outstrip the ability of a democratic government to utilize them and to contain them within the framework of a democratic society.

There are no simple prescriptions but it is certain that government in all areas must be prepared to meet the challenges. Americans must equip all of the branches of government to their utmost capacity to perform, particularly the branch that principally distinguishes a democracy from a dictatorship—the legislature.

Index